NEWNES ALL COLOUR GUIDE
WINDSURFING

NEWNES ALL COLOUR GUIDE
WINDSURFING

STEPHEN TURNER

NEWNES BOOKS

Dedication

To Gaynor, without whom this book would
not have been written.

Acknowledgements

I would like to thank the following for their help and advice in the
preparation of this book:
Peter and Dee Caldwell, Cliff Webb, Roger and John Tushingham, Lester Noble,
Deirdre Keegan, Peter Ens, Groom & Pickerill.
My special thanks go to Simon Bornhoft and Paula Wickens
for appearing in most of the photographs.
Thanks are also due to Club Mistral, The Caribbean Alternative,
The Barbados Windsurfing Club, British West Indian Airways,
Dee Caldwell's Sailboard Centre, Princes Windsurfing,
Windsurfers' World, Bears Board Repair, Tushingham Sails
and Gul Wetsuits.
Photographs by Cliff Webb.
Additional photographs by Alex Williams
and Stephen Turner.

Published by Newnes Books,
a Division of The Hamlyn Publishing Group Limited
Bridge House, 69 London Road, Twickenham,
Middlesex, England
and distributed for them by Hamlyn Distribution
Services Limited, Rushden, Northants, England.

Text © copyright Stephen J. Turner 1986
Illustrations © Newnes Books,
a Division of The Hamlyn Publishing Group Limited 1986

Designed by Groom & Pickerill

ISBN 0 600 35889 5
Printed in Italy

CONTENTS

INTRODUCTION

Some pastimes are merely temporary fads, but once in a while something is invented that instantly captures the imagination and, as time passes, establishes itself as a genuinely new sport.

Windsurfing is one such sport. It was invented in 1969, yet has grown so rapidly it now enjoys official Olympic status, has millions of followers around the world and has given rise to a multi-million dollar industry.

What, then, has given this unusual mixture of sailing and surfing its own identity and made it so popular? If you were to ask ten windsurfing enthusiasts you would probably get ten different answers. Some would say it is because it is easy, convenient, fun-filled and even relaxing; others would describe it as a challenging and exhilarating sport that requires considerable skill and a competitive spirit. Some sailors own just one board and sail on their local lake or a nearby sheltered bay, but others own four or five specialist boards and travel the world in search of strong winds and huge waves. The fact is that windsurfing is really great fun and can be enjoyed by anyone.

In the beginning

A sailboard is little more than a surfboard with a sail attached. A simple idea, but because a board with a fixed mast and sail is impossible to balance, it took the invention of what is known as the *free-sail* system to make it work. This consists of a two-sided *wishbone* boom that can be used to hold onto both sides of the sail, and a universal joint at the base of the mast that allows it to be moved in any direction. In this way the sailor can balance his weight against the pull of the sail.

In a 1965 issue of the American magazine *Popular Science Monthly*, an unambitious inventor called Newman Darby wrote an article describing his invention of a new sport based very crudely on a free-sail system. His craft incorporated a square-rigger type of sail which partially pivoted in its mast socket. Although a few were made and sold, the Newman Darby sailboard never really attracted any further attention.

It was two Californians, Jim Drake and Hoyle Schweitzer, who are generally credited with the invention of the sailboard as we know it today. Necessity is the mother of invention, as the saying goes, and both Drake and Schweitzer had good reason to need a craft that worked along the lines of a modern sailboard. Drake was a keen sailor but was fed up with the complicated and time-consuming rigging procedure that was required by his sailing dinghy, especially with the limited amount of free time his job as an aeronautical engineer allowed him. He wanted something that was convenient to use and maintain. For his part, Schweitzer was a keen surfer but hated the exhausting paddle out to sea that was always required before he could surf the waves back onto the beach. In 1967 Drake met Schweitzer and the two began cooperating on solving each other's problem. By August 1969, Drake was ready to present a paper on the invention of a new free-sailing system to a symposium on sailboat design held by the American Institute of Aeronautics and Astronautics.

Meanwhile Schweitzer, who was the entrepreneur of the partnership, had realized that there was considerable commercial potential in a free-sailing craft and had taken out a patent on the design in as many countries as possible. Within a year of Drake's paper, he had put the design into production and began selling the world's first sailboards. The very first Windsurfers, as they were named, were hand-made but it wasn't long before Schweitzer began mass-producing them in a new man-made plastic called polyethylene.

With great foresight, Schweitzer not only patented the Windsurfer in the United States, but also filed patent applications in Canada, Australia, Japan and various European countries, including Britain, Germany and Holland. It was the patent, which placed severe restrictions on the manufacture of sailboards and related equipment by non-licensees, that gave rise to claims by others that they, rather than Hoyle Schweitzer, were the first to invent the sailboard.

Europe and the patent

Oddly enough, windsurfing remained little more than a minor craze in California during the early seventies, but in Europe the new sport gained popularity at a rate even the confident Schweitzer had not dared dream of.

By 1970, Schweitzer had bought out Jim Drake's half of the partnership for just a few thousand dollars (much to Drake's subsequent regret). He left his position as vice-president of a computer service company and began to concentrate on his new business, which at that time was still based in his garage and living room! In his search for new markets for the Windsurfer, Schweitzer came across a large Dutch textile corporation called Nijverdal Ten Cate. The company began to import the boards into Europe where, to everyone's surprise, they began to sell in numbers previously unheard of. In 1973 a new company called Ten Cate Sports was formed to manufacture Windsurfers under licence in Europe and by 1975 sales had risen to over 5000.

The bandwagon was soon rolling, the sport gained popularity rapidly and by 1980 scores of different brands had appeared on the market in Europe. Apart from Ten Cate's Windsurfer, the big brands were HiFly, Sailboard and Wind-

Windsurfing: a sport anyone can enjoy.

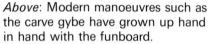
Above: Modern manoeuvres such as the carve gybe have grown up hand in hand with the funboard.

The first boards

Top and above: The pioneering sailors and designers of Hawaii have had a profound influence on modern windsurfing. And the 'waveboards' first built for the excellent jumping and wave-riding conditions to be found in Hawaii are the direct ancestors of today's funboards.

glider (Germany), Dufour (France) and Mistral (Switzerland).

Schweitzer, however, was determined to enjoy the benefits of his foresight and began to pursue the unlicensed manufacturers through the courts for the infringement of his patent.

France was one of the major sailboarding nations in which he had neglected to file a patent, but in Germany his lawyers had more success, forcing such well-known brand names as Mistral to accept a licensing agreement in 1981 and pay the required $7\frac{1}{2}$ per cent royalty fees.

Early claimants

Other manufacturers in other countries were to follow suit but in 1982 a small British importer of unlicensed sailboards from France, Tabur Marine, decided to make a stand when taken to court by Schweitzer's lawyers. During the court hearings a witness for the defence claimed that he had invented and used a sailboard on the south coast of England in 1958 while he was still a teenager. His name was Peter Chilvers and to everyone's amazement, the judge upheld his claim. Legally, and despite subsequent appeals from Schweitzer's lawyers, he became the inventor of the sailboard as far as Britain was concerned.

In Australia an almost identical case was heard in front of a Sydney judge in 1984. This time it was a man called Richard Eastaugh who claimed to have first used a free-sail system in Sydney Harbour shortly after the end of World War II. The judge accepted his evidence and Schweitzer's Australian patent was held to be invalid.

Of course, the real history of windsurfing – the story of how the sport developed among its real enthusiasts – is far removed from patents, lawcourts and royalty payments. How did Drake and Schweitzer's original Windsurfer give rise to all the numerous facets of windsurfing today?

Windsurfing is a sport that requires a particular brand of dynamic balance and so demands that the sailor develop certain skills before he can use his equipment effectively. At the outset, no one possessed these skills and so all boards were made to be stable and easy to sail in all directions. The original Windsurfer was ideal from that point of view and most early boards were merely variations on a theme. It wasn't until the mid-seventies that even the first proper teaching system was devised by a certain Dagobert Benz on behalf of Hoyle Schweitzer's company, Windsurfing International Inc.

As it incorporated a sail and was, for the most part, subject to normal sailing 'theory', windsurfing was regarded as just another type of dinghy sailing (much more so than it is today). So, it not only borrowed conventional sailing terms (tacking, gybing, sheeting in and out and so on), it also utilized the same basic competition format, 'Olympic' triangle racing.

It was not surprising, therefore, that when the time came to redesign boards in order to enhance their performance on the racing circuit in the late seventies, high-performance boards began to bear a slight resemblance to yacht-racing hulls. These boards, although too unstable for beginners, were very fast in light winds and on flat water and became known as 'displacement boards': displacement because they cut through the water with

their rounded or 'V'-shaped hulls rather than skimming across it on flat ones.

At the turn of the decade the typical boardsailor was faced with the choice of sticking to his basic, flat board or opting for the faster, but more expensive, 'round' displacement board for use in International Yacht Racing Union (IYRU) Division II racing. (Most flat boards could be raced in Division I.)

Meanwhile, in Hawaii, the sport was taking a radically different direction. The Hawaiian islands produce spectacular windsurfing conditions. Wind is channelled through the narrow, deep valleys that divide Hawaii's many steep-sided volcanic mountains to whistle out over the huge, smooth-faced rolling waves that thunder in unhindered from the Pacific. Faced with these conditions, local boardsailors, tired of hiding from the elements in sheltered bays, began to adapt their equipment to cope with them.

The single most influential development of the time was the invention of the footstrap by Larry Stanley in 1977. Although a simple accessory, the footstrap revolutionized sailing techniques as it allowed the sailor to remain in contact with his board whatever happened – even when the two were in mid-air following a jump. Boards became shorter and lighter, to produce the manoeuvrability that the newly skilled 'riders' required and the experience of traditional surfboard shapers, rather than that of yacht designers, was called upon to produce the new generation of high-wind, high-performance 'waveboards'.

Funboards

Developments in Hawaii did not go unnoticed by the Europeans and others around the world. Enthusiastic sailors, many of whom were disillusioned with the traditional racing circuits (which had become immersed in burdensome measurement rules), began to search for new windsurfing challenges and took up Hawaiian-style short-board sailing, using specially built custom boards.

The major manufacturers were also looking for new opportunities and began to exploit the new style of sailing favoured by the experts. Unfortunately, short waveboards were unsuitable for the mass market as they were difficult to sail and required quite extreme conditions to really perform well. A compromise was soon hit upon: a board that was relatively easy to sail but one that also had some of the high-performance attributes of a shorter, less stable board. The all-round funboard was born.

The first funboards appeared on the market in mass production form in 1981 and 1982. Some were hit-and-miss affairs in design terms but the less efficient soon fell by the wayside. The rig (the mast, sail and boom combination) was also improved to match the easy handling yet high-performance characteristics of these modern boards. Today the term funboard covers a wide variety of boards, referring to all boards, short or long, that are designed to excel in higher winds of around Force 4 (11–16 knots) and more, yet can still be sailed by the average sailor in less demanding conditions.

With the funboard revolution a new windsurfing vocabulary was born to describe the new sailing methods: foot-steering, carve gybing, water starting and so on. These are all now well-established funboard techniques. To complement these new skills, funboard competition rules, some unique to windsurfing, were formulated. These included slaloms, ins-and-outs (of surf), wave-riding contests, funboard course racing, speed trials and long-distance marathons.

Windsurfing today

Funboards of one kind or another dominate the windsurfing scene today but the more traditional forms of windsurfing are still holding their own. Simple, recreational sailing is the most common, of course, but freestyle, the sport's gymnastic side, is a favourite of many sailors, especially as it requires only a basic board and a light wind.

Alongside funboard competition, which is now well-established on both a professional and an amateur level, conventional triangle racing continues to flourish around the world and was the format used for the 1984 Olympic Games in Los Angeles – boardsailing's first Olympics. Even this branch of windsurfing has its different types. There are three divisions (including tandems) of open-class racing run by the International Yacht Racing Union, and a number of 'one-design' class associations that hold regional, national and international championships for sailors of a particular model of board.

The modern sporting man's desire to excel in all areas is not lacking in the boardsailor. Speed trials have established speeds of well over 30 knots. In endurance trials sailors have sailed continuously for over three whole days.

Below: Some early boards: in the background is an original Windsurfer and lying next to it is the first production waveboard. This was merely a standard Windsurfer fitted with footstraps and with a daggerboard moved aft. Other boards designed specifically for high winds soon followed (centre) and it wasn't long before these 'funboards' became so small and manoeuvrable that the shortest hadn't enough buoyancy to keep the sailor and the rig afloat unless travelling at speed. These became known as 'sinkers'.

Sailors have sailed in near-hurricane force winds, around islands and icebergs, and one intrepid and brave Frenchman, Christian Marty, has even sailed across the Atlantic, eating and sleeping on his board.

Feats of strength and endurance aside, windsurfing is a sport for all ages and abilities: there are special boards for young children and, at the other end of the spectrum, sixty years and over is still not too old for qualification as an instructor!

Preparation and technique, rather than brute strength and daring, are the keynotes to successful windsurfing. Whether you are looking for solitude and quiet relaxation as a light-weather recreational sailor, or for sheer excitement and exhilaration as you rip through a wave on your funboard, you will find that windsurfing has something to offer.

How to use this book

For the novice, and even the experienced sailor, the windsurfing world can be a confusing place. Apart from having to learn how to 'do it standing up' with all the tacking, gybing, running and reaching that that involves, he or she is faced with a good deal of jargon, an alarming number of bits and pieces for such a deceptively simple craft, and seemingly numerous types of boards, sails, techniques, racing classes and competitions.

This book sets out to clarify the windsurfing scene: the equipment, the techniques, the competitions and the jargon. It is divided into four parts, the first three covering each of the ability levels and their associated equipment and techniques, while the fourth part looks at the important aspect of windsurfing safety (water can be dangerous!), freestyle and the often confusing area of competitive windsurfing.

Bottom: Schweitzer's original Windsurfer remains one of the most popular boards of today.

BASIC
WINDSURFING

Apart from the excitement and exhilaration of harnessing the wind on such a small craft as a sailboard, the major attraction of windsurfing is its simplicity. All the necessary equipment can be transported on top of a car and only the frailest of adults would have difficulty in carrying a board to the water's edge.

It is on the water that the real benefits become evident. Once the board and rig have been put together, no further adjustment is needed. The sailor simply balances his own weight against the force of the wind in the sail and off he goes, steering, accelerating, and decelerating with subtle movements of his arms and body.

Given the right conditions and good instruction, there is no reason why the novice boardsailor should not acquire a basic ability to sail in a single day. Many people fail to learn in a day because they use inappropriate equipment, because the conditions are not suitable, or because they are not aware of the basic principles of boardsailing. A proper course of instruction is highly recommended, as it will make the sometimes painful task of learning to sail quicker, easier and, above all, safer.

If you are taught by a friend, make sure that he teaches you the important safety aspects of windsurfing. You will find these in a special section towards the end of this book (pages 86–89). Learn them, practise them and remember them. On the whole windsurfing is a safe sport – but only for those who know how to keep it safe.

Given the right conditions of flat water, light winds and good instruction, there is no reason why the beginner should not learn the basics of windsurfing in a day or two.

EQUIPMENT AND THEORY

Essentially, the sailboard has seven constituent parts: the hull (the board itself) to which is attached a daggerboard (centreboard) and a skeg (fin); and a rig that consists of a mast, a sail and a boom; the seventh and all-important part is the universal joint (or UJ), which connects the board to the rig and allows the latter to move freely in all directions.

In addition to these seven basic parts are bits and pieces of rope that hold the rig together and other attachments that are not always necessary but enhance the board's performance in some way. These consist of such things as footstraps, mast tracks, harness lines, battens and extra fins. Initially, the beginner need not concern himself with most of these as they will only serve to complicate matters.

Left to right: The different types of sailboard: a 390cm (12ft 7in) high-volume displacement board; a standard 380cm (12ft 4in) flatboard (note the lack of footstraps); an all-round funboard (this one is 370cm (12ft 1in) long and could probably be sailed by an ambitious first-timer); a medium-length funboard (some boards of this length, around 320–330cm (10ft 4in–10ft 8in), have daggerboards and some don't); a marginal funboard 290cm long (9ft 5in); and an outright sinker only 255cm (8ft 3in) long.

Boards

Boards can be bought in a variety of sizes and shapes in order to cater for different wind and water conditions and sailors of different ability levels. Boards themselves are differentiated by their lengths, 3.9m (12ft 7in) being the longest you will find. The majority of boards are around 3.6m to 3.8m (11ft 8in to 12ft 4in) long but high-performance boards can be as short as 2.4m (7ft 8in).

Length is used to categorize boards because it is a good guide to the amount of volume in a board. Along with the precise shape of a board it is volume (i.e. the amount of water it displaces when totally

Length, volume and hull design each has an influence on how a board behaves on the water. The board on the left, a displacement board designed for light-wind racing, has a rounded hull for good upwind speed; the board in the middle has a flat hull for stability; and the board on the right has a modern 'concave' hull for quick acceleration and fast reaching.

submerged) and the way it is distributed that really governs a board's behaviour on the water. A long board with plenty of volume distributed evenly along its length and across its width will tend to be stable and easy to sail. On the other hand, a short board with very little volume (and hence weight) will be easy to manoeuvre at speed but will be very unstable for a sailor with no experience. In extreme cases, a sinker will not support the weight of the sailor and the rig unless it is planing (that is, skimming across the water rather than merely moving through it).

Too much volume, or more specifically volume in the wrong place, can also make a board unstable. The displacement boards used for light-wind racing have plenty of length and volume but their hulls are rounded or sometimes 'V' shaped. This makes them sit high in the water and so are too unstable for the first-time sailor.

The ideal board for a novice sailor should be long (about 3.7m–3.8m (12ft 1 in–12ft 4in), fairly wide (a minimum of 65cms (13.7in) at its widest point) and should have sufficient volume for its weight (the average adult would need 230–260 litres).

The more stable and 'raft-like' a board is, the better it will be for the very first stages of windsurfing. However, if you are thinking of buying a board on which you hope to progress, it would be wise to choose a slightly less stable board with more performance potential. This may make things difficult at first but you will not get bored after just a few weeks.

Board shapes

In the early days of board design all boards had relatively flat hulls and slightly rounded or square tails (sterns). Today, board design has become more sophisticated with most boards being subtle compromises between different performance-orientated design features and that all-important factor, stability.

The most important parts of a board to the designer are those in contact with the water: namely, the underside of the hull, the sides (rails) and the rear (the tail). The first boards to break away from the flat-hull/squared-tail mould of the early boards were the displacement boards designed for IYRU Division II triangle racing at the end of the 1970s. As triangle racing is won and lost on the upwind legs, the displacement board was designed to have a long waterline length. This helps it to bite into the water along its whole length and sail upwind easily in light to moderate winds. Despite the huge volume needed to achieve this (over 300 litres) displacement boards are light because they have a hollow hull. They are also fragile and difficult to sail.

At the same time, waveboards – the forerunners of the modern funboard –

were being developed in Hawaii under the auspices of the big European manufacturers. The first waveboards were small and light for the time and had huge round and voluminous tails designed to produce lift for quick planing (acceleration) and jumping. It was soon realized, however, that a thinner, sharper tail that allowed the sailor to sink the rear end of the board and grip the water during a high-speed turn was a much more desirable shape.

Apart from the overall length and width considerations mentioned earlier, nearly all modern funboards are a compromise between volume and width in the tail for easy planing and jumping, and narrow, thin tails for easy turning.

Rails became hard (i.e. sharp) at the rear end of the board to increase grip on the water but remained soft (i.e. rounded) further up the board, so that they wouldn't catch during a turn.

Once the designers had sorted out the tail of the funboard, attention turned to the underside of the hull which, apart from the 'rocker' (curvature) in the front section, needed to keep the nose from ploughing in the waves, had always been flat. The bottom contours, as they are known, of modern boards are now quite advanced hydrodynamically. Single, double and even triple 'concave' hulls, air scoops and channels are now common hull features intended to reduce drag and increase lift, thereby increasing speed and acceleration respectively.

Board construction

Sailboards are made in one of three different materials: polyethylene, ABS plastic (or its derivative ASA) or GRP (glass reinforced plastic). Some manufacturers use other materials such as Unitene or Copex for example, but these are brand-named variations on one or other of the basic three construction materials. Although some of these may be marginal improvements, they will still be subject to the same advantages and disadvantages of each base material.

Polyethylene boards can either be roto-moulded or blow-moulded. Roto-moulding involves heating polyethylene chips in a mould that is then rotated at speed so that the molten polyethylene forms a skin on the inside of the mould. Blow-moulding involves injecting compressed air into a tube of hot polyethylene inside a mould in order to form a skin. The skins are then filled with liquid poly-urethane foam, which hardens inside to make the resultant board stiff and watertight.

The main advantage of making a board in polyethylene is that it is a tough and durable material and the con-

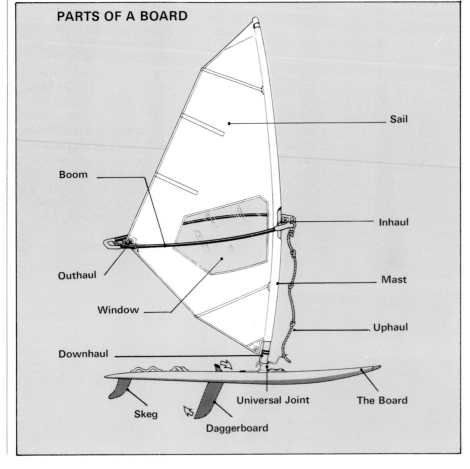

PARTS OF A BOARD

Sail
Boom
Inhaul
Outhaul
Mast
Window
Uphaul
Downhaul
Skeg
Universal Joint
The Board
Daggerboard

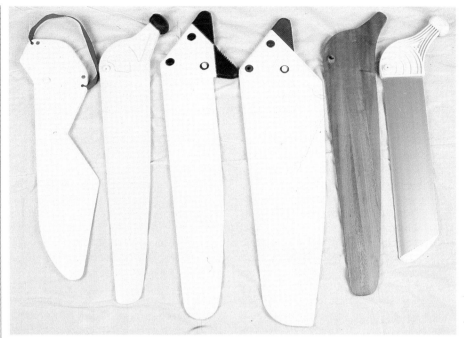

struction process leaves no seams that could leak. However, polyethylene boards are heavier and less stiff than other boards and do not have the same smooth finish as ASA and GRP boards.

Boards made in ABS or its close relative ASA (which is now much more common) are made in a slightly different manner. Two sheets of plastic, one for the deck and one for the underside of the hull, are moulded separately and then glued together to form the skin. Polyurethane or polystyrene foam is used to form the core of the board. The benefits of ABS and ASA are that they result in a better cosmetic finish and a stiffer (and therefore faster) board. The ABS/ASA construction method also makes it possible for stringers (strengthening bars) to be fitted inside the board. However, ABS/ASA boards are less durable than polyethylene and they can leak at the seams.

The GRP construction process is the oldest method of board construction (it has been used to make standard surfboards since the late 1950s) but it is also the one in which the most recent developments have taken place. At its most basic level, GRP is used to make custom boards and the techniques and materials required are by no means beyond the scope of the average do-it-yourself enthusiast. At the other end of the spectrum, the GRP process is used to produce the most advanced 'high-tech' boards on the market.

A pre-shaped polystyrene 'blank' is taken and covered with glass fibre cloth. The cloth is impregnated with a plastic resin which is then left to harden before a finishing 'gel coat' is applied. A custom-board builder would 'shape' the blank and 'lay up' the cloth and resin himself,

leaving the skin to dry in the open air. The larger-scale brand manufacturers use a machine-shaped blank, lay up the cloth and resin inside a mould and bake the board for extra strength and stiffness.

This process has numerous variations, the most common being the use of epoxy resin instead of the standard polyester resin. Epoxy produces a lighter, stiffer board – the modern 'epoxy' board. Different amounts and types of cloth (Kevlar is a common substitute) can be used to alter the final weight, strength, durability and, of course, price of the final product.

GRP and epoxy boards lend themselves to high-performance sailing as they tend to be light, stiff and have smooth, fast underwater surfaces. However, they are also expensive and easily damaged. The newcomer to windsurfing should keep to polyethylene or ASA boards and leave GRP and epoxy boards to the experts.

Parts of a board

The daggerboard

The purpose of a daggerboard (centreboard) is to provide the board with lateral resistance – in other words, to stop it slipping sideways through the water. It also gives the board extra stability, making it harder to tip it over – especially when the board is at rest.

There are three types of daggerboard: the standard straight daggerboard, which can be either 'up' or 'down'; the pivoting daggerboard, which pivots back and forth in its slot, altering the position (but not the amount) of lateral resistance beneath the board; and the fully retracting daggerboard, which can be totally withdrawn and housed inside the hull. The latter type is by far the most popular and

Top left: Different types of daggerboard: the dagger on the left is an old-fashioned pivoting daggerboard. To its right are three types of modern fully retracting dagger, the third one being extra wide for maximum lateral resistance when sailing upwind. Most daggerboards are made of moulded plastic but the two racing daggers on the right are made of wood and aluminium for extra rigidity when travelling at speed.

Top right: A typical skeg (or fin). Note the torpedo-shaped protrusions. They are there to prevent aerated water flowing down the skeg which could otherwise lose its grip in a fast turn.

Above right: There are many different designs of mast foot and universal joint (UJ). The photo illustrates a spring-loaded UJ (far left), a mechanical or hinged UJ (centre) and various types of hour-glass-shaped rubber 'power joints' and mast feet.

common today. Daggerboards only appear on boards longer than 3 to 3.2m (10ft–10ft 6in) long.

The skeg

The skeg simply stops the back of the board slipping sideways. That is, it provides the board with directional stability. Sailing a board without a skeg would be almost impossible as the board would continually slide away from beneath your feet.

Made of polycarbonate (plastic) or hand-crafted GRP, skegs come in a variety of shapes and sizes but all are

Below: Mast tracks come in a variety of shapes and sizes. Nearly all are adjustable at sea except those of the 'skeg-box' variety (left) which must be positioned on shore.

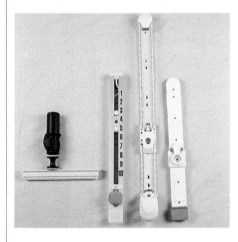

Below: A loop of rope attached to the towing eye and a rubber nose bumper are useful safety features.

designed to reduce the possibility of 'spin out' occuring. This is a phenomenon that occurs at speed, in a fast turn or on landing from a jump when the skeg loses its grip in the water due to excessive aeration. Spin out is something the average sailor probably will not experience until he has become a skilled short-board sailor.

The mast foot and universal joint

The universal joint (UJ) is the device that makes a sailboard so different from other forms of sailing craft as it allows the rig to swing round 360 degrees and to incline up to 180 degrees (or more) towards the water.

The UJ itself can come in three different forms: the mechanical UJ consists of either a twin-hinge arrangement, one hinge working on the horizontal plane and the other on the vertical plane; or on a spring-loaded nylon cord, which allows the rig to fall in any direction. The most common type of UJ, however, is the revolving 'power-joint', an hour-glass-

shaped piece of reinforced rubber that turns and bends in the desired direction under the weight of the rig.

Underneath the universal joint is the mast foot. This device attaches the UJ and the rig to the board. Mast feet should keep the rig locked to the board under normal sailing conditions but should give way under extreme pressure – when your leg is trapped between the mast and the board after a fall, for example.

There are many types of mast feet available but most use a pressure/friction system or a twin-pronged pin that will expand and release the mast foot from the board under pressure. A mast foot that continually pops out can be annoying and some sailors prefer a system that locks in. These systems are not uncommon but they are less safe than mast feet that release under pressure. The mast foot/universal joint arrangement should also allow for the attachment of a safety leash. This prevents the board and rig parting company should the mast foot come out while you are on the water.

The mast-foot well and mast track

The mast-foot well is the circular or 'T' shaped slot in the board into which the mast foot is placed. Most boards will have an alternative well to give the sailor a choice of two positions. The spare well is then frequently used to secure the safety leash. (The alternative point on the board to which the safety leash can be attached is the towing eye.)

Twin and even triple mast-foot wells can be limiting and many modern boards are supplied with mast tracks instead.

These allow the sailor to move the rig back and forth while he is on the water and so select his preferred mast position. (See Using an Adjustable Mast Track, page 44.)

Each mast track on the market works in a slightly different manner. Most use a foot-operated pedal-release system, whereas others adjust manually, or are continuously adjustable or have a number of fixed positions. All tracks have one thing in common though – they are prone to clogging up with sand.

Mast tracks are an undoubted advantage to a sailor who knows how to use them, but the beginner should avoid them. If you have one on the board you are learning on, then keep it in a fixed, central position and ignore it.

Footstraps

Footstraps were once regarded as suitable for experts only. Nowadays straps, or footstrap fittings, are supplied on all but the most basic boards. Their purpose is simply to keep the sailor properly in contact with his board at high speeds.

Beginners should ignore straps as they will only get in the way and should preferably use a board that has none. On the other hand it is useful to buy a board to which straps can be fitted. This will make progression to funboard sailing an easier task. If the straps themselves are supplied, make sure that they are not only comfortable but adjustable as well. Badly fitting footstraps are dangerous.

The towing eye and bumper

For safety reasons, all boards have towing eyes near the nose, to which rope can be attached in case the board needs to be towed to the shore for any reason.

Although many boards don't have one, a soft rubber nose bumper is a good idea. Not only will it help to prevent damage to the nose of your board should you hit an obstruction, it will also cause a lot less damage to the obstruction – and that could be a swimmer or another sailor.

Non-slip

In order to offer an effective grip for the sailor's feet, part of the board's deck is given a specially textured surface called the non-slip area. This should extend at least 60cm (2ft) in front of the mast on a long board. Sometimes, the non-slip wears away or is rendered useless by suntan oil. This can be corrected with the use of a special wax or the non-slip itself can be reapplied by a board repairer.

Left: A typical double 'Y' footstrap arrangement allowing for two front-foot positions and three back-foot positions.

The Rig

The rig is the engine-room of the free-sailing system, harnessing the energy of the wind and converting it into lift and forward drive.

An explanation of the theory behind a sailboard rig would fill a book in itself. But, to put it simply, the sail acts rather like an aircraft's wing. When the wind meets the mast, the airflow separates and flows across the curved surface of the sail faster on the leeward (the sheltered or downwind) side than it does over the windward side (the surface closer to the source of the wind). This happens because the air particles have further to travel on the leeward side.

When the air particles accelerate over the leeward surface the pressure is reduced and the rig is 'sucked' along as the higher pressure on the windward side moves to equalize the difference. The fact that the air flows over the sail, instead of simply blowing into it and pushing it along, means that the sailboard can be sailed at quite a close angle to the wind. Resistance sailing, as it is called, only occurs on a run when the sailboard is heading straight downwind. In this case the wind blows into the sail, spilling out on all sides, and doesn't require a daggerboard to provide any lateral resistance.

The rig itself consists of a mast (the leading edge), a sail and a 'wishbone' boom. It is important when buying or replacing any of these to ensure that they match. For example, different sails are suited to masts of different 'stiffness' ratings. Unless the two match it will be difficult to 'set' the sail properly without creases. Mast extensions can be added to masts that are too short for a sail. However, a mast that is too long will leave a large gap between the sail and the board making the whole rig inefficient. The boom should match the width of the sail: too short and it will be useless, too long and the rig will be unbalanced and the boom may drag in the water.

Sail materials

All sails are constructed of man-made materials (in fact, of different forms of polyester). In its fibrous form polyester is woven to form a cloth, the most common being Dacron. (Dacron and its equivalents, Terylene, Teteron etc., are all trade names for polyester cloth). It can also be extruded in sheet form to be used as a very thin film or laminate, as in the case of Mylar (Mylar and Melinex are trade names for polyester laminates).

At one time nearly all sails were made of polyester cloth. It is relatively cheap, durable and easy to work with, but it has

the disadvantage of stretching with use and becoming permanently distorted. This is not much use to the sailmaker who takes great pride and care in designing a sail with a certain shape and profile, or to the sailor who finds that his sail becomes harder and harder to manage the more he uses it.

Mylar, on the other hand, being a film rather than a cloth, doesn't stretch and so Dacron sails destined for high-performance use were laminated on one side with Mylar. This was only a limited improvement, however, as the Dacron side of the sail still retained water (increasing its weight) and the Mylar side was prone to delamination. Mylar itself also has its disadvantages: it is expensive and tears very easily as it has no inherent strength.

The solution more recently hit upon by sailmakers is to laminate Mylar onto both sides of a scrim material (material woven like a mesh). The Mylar doesn't stretch or hold water and the scrim prevents the Mylar from tearing easily. Today, cheaper sails are still made out of Dacron or the other cloths, while more expensive, specialist or high-wind sails are made of

On the left is a high-performance sail made of a polyester laminate. Note the full-length battens and short boom. On the right is a standard, short-battened 'soft' sail made of polyester cloth.

scrim Mylar or a combination of Dacron and scrim-Mylar panels.

Sail design

The essence of sail design is to build the desired amount of 'fullness' into the sail. Full sails have a deep 'draught' and so produce extra power. Flat sails are shallow and sacrifice power to controllability. The crucial factor in sail design, however, is the position and the stability of the 'centre of effort' (CE) – an imaginary point on the sail representing the sum of all the forces acting upon it. Whether the sail is set flat or full, the further forward the point of maximum draught (and hence the further forward the centre of effort) the easier the sail will be to handle.

The whole rig is prone to bending and flexing as it is hit by gusts of wind and as

Mast extensions come in a variety of sizes. Some models (such as the three on the right) are adjustable.

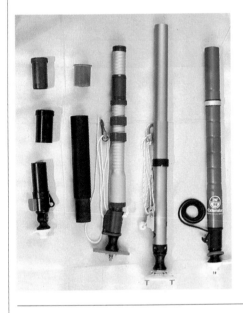

the board travels through waves. This will cause the CE to move around, making it difficult for the sailor to remain in complete control.

By cutting and stitching each panel of the sail together in a certain way, the sailmaker can position the centre of effort in a particular area and then keep it there with the use of battens, stiff masts and non-stretch materials such as Mylar.

In addition to the fullness built into the sail the sailmaker is interested in its 'aspect ratio'. This is the ratio of a sail's mast height to its boom length. When board-sailors first began to sail in large waves, the boom and the 'clew' end of the sail would drag in the waves. It was also discovered that the top section of the sail (the head), which was pointed, was prone to stalling and decreased the overall performance of the sail.

In endeavouring to solve these problems, sailmakers found that a sail with a fatter head area but an overall taller, thinner profile had certain advantages: none of the sail area was wasted, the sail was easier to uphaul and didn't drag in the water when the sail was underway, and when combined with the new materials and full-length battens, the sail could be made much more stable and wing-like.

Today, most sails of a particular size have higher aspect ratios than those of days gone by, the only limiting factor

being the elasticity of the materials used. The high tension required to rig these sails would soon ruin a Dacron sail, for example.

There are many other aspects of sail design a sailmaker has to consider: the type of leading edge to be used; the type and number of battens the sail requires; how to maintain stability in the 'leach' area of the sail; how to reinforce the various areas of the sail under high tension without excessively increasing the overall weight of the sail; and so on. Although all of these factors are of interest to an expert sailor, the beginner need only ensure that his sail is of the correct size and is not blown out (stretched). Such sails allow the point of maximum draught, and hence the centre of effort, to move back in strong winds or during a gust and this can make them hard to handle.

However, if you are buying a sail consider carefully whether Mylar sails or sails with high-performance designs are really for you – Mylar sails require a great deal of care and attention and aero-dynamically advanced sails may be too 'unforgiving' for the beginner. (See the section on high-performance equipment.) Make sure the sail is well made. Examine the stitching and look at the amount of reinforcement in the head, tack and clew areas. Is the window in the right position? Is it possible to rig the sail without creases? And, above all, is it the right size?

SAILS

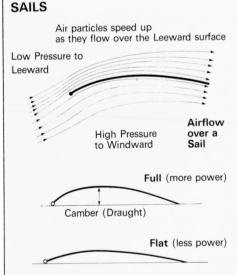

Air particles speed up as they flow over the Leeward surface

Low Pressure to Leeward

High Pressure to Windward

Airflow over a Sail

Full (more power)

Camber (Draught)

Flat (less power)

1 A sail with a high aspect ratio (solid line) compared to a sail with a low aspect ratio (dotted line).

Sail profiles—
Types of sail: not all sails fall neatly into categories. The following types are therefore just a rough indication of what is available:

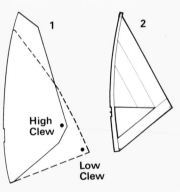

High Clew

Low Clew

2 *Pinheads:* generally smaller than 4sq m (45sq ft) and suited to beginners, children and strong winds.

3 & 4 *Powerheads:* standard sails (4–7sq m: 45–75sq ft) with a full-length head batten and two or three leech battens. Larger, more modern versions may have one or two foot battens to stabilize the extra area in the sail. Powerheads are normally made of polyester cloth (although some may feature Mylar panels) and are suited to all-round use.

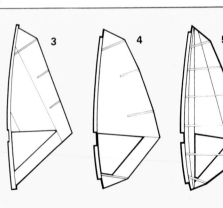

5 *Fully battened sails:* these are nearly always high-performance sails featuring Mylar materials and sophisticated leading edges (see pages 56 and 57 for details of rotationals, camber inducers etc.) They come in all sizes from 3sq m (30sq ft) to 8sq m (90sq ft) or more and are generally designed to suit a particular purpose, for example wave sailing, speed sailing or racing. The full-length battens and light, low-stretch materials used in these sails make them powerful yet stable and easy to handle in high winds.

Sail size

Life was a good deal easier for the early boardsailor faced only with the choice of which sail to buy or use in a given wind strength. He either opted for his standard, full-sized sail or he rigged a storm sail, which was smaller and less powerful.

Today, both design and materials influence the amount of power in a sail but size remains the single most important governing factor and the choice is very much wider than it used to be. Choosing the wrong size and being underpowered is frustrating and can make sailing difficult, but choosing the wrong size and being overpowered can be dangerous. Beginners should always use a small sail (under 59sq ft – 5.5sq m) until they learn how to handle a board properly.

The exact size of the sail you choose to use on a particular day will depend on the wind strength, your own strength, weight and ability, and the design of the sail itself. In practice, a sailor of average build and ability should easily be able to cope with a standard 'powerhead' 7.5sq m (81sq ft) standard powerhead sail in winds of up to Force 3 (7–10 knots) but would have difficulty handling a 5.5sq m (59sq ft) or a 6sq m (65sq ft) sail in a Force 5–6 wind (17–27kn). Sails can be as large as 9sq m (97sq ft) or even 10sq m (108sq ft) and as small as 3.2sq m (35sq ft).

Depending on the number you can afford, an ideal 'quiver' of three sails might include a 7sq m (76sq ft) for light winds and racing, 5–6sq m (54–65sq ft) for funboard sailing in winds of around Force 4 (11–16kn) and a storm sail, perhaps 4.5sq m (49sq ft) or less, for much higher winds.

The mast and mast extension

The mast fits into the luff sleeve (or tube) on the sail and is attached to the board by means of the universal joint. Because the mast puts tension into the sail along with the boom, its stiffness rating is important. This is measured using the German Din rating: 7.1 would indicate a relatively stiff mast.

Masts are made in either GRP (epoxy), the most common material, or in aluminium. Aluminium masts are used primarily for racing as they are very stiff and so transfer power from the sail to the board very efficiently. This also makes them vulnerable to breakage, especially in waves.

Rather than have a mast that will accommodate your tallest sail and so leave a large gap between the board and the foot of the sail when you fit your smallest sail, you can use an adjustable mast extension to alter the height of the mast as required. Mast extensions are added to the base of the mast and are supplied as standard fittings with most modern funboards.

The boom

Conventional booms have been standard fittings on sailing craft for centuries but the wishbone (i.e. two-sided) boom is unique to windsurfing. Booms are made of shaped alloy tubing held together at either end by hard plastic or metal 'boom ends', which incorporate cleats and pulleys for rigging purposes. Booms are covered in either vulcanized rubber or a more comfortable sponge-like rubber 'grip'.

As sails are made in different sizes and shapes, some booms are adjustable so that they can be used with more than one sail: a rig with an excessively long boom will be unbalanced and inefficient. These booms can be adjusted either telescopically or with the use of a number of removable sections fitted to the outhaul end.

The important factors to look for in a boom are stiffness, ease of adjustment and lightness – some booms are filled with foam to prevent them filling with water. Well-designed end fittings to booms will make rigging and sailing more efficient as well.

The inhaul, outhaul and downhaul

These are the short lengths of rope used to hold the rig together. (See the section on rigging.) The inhaul connects the boom to the mast, while the outhaul connects the other (clew) end of the boom to the sail and is used to put tension into the rig horizontally. The downhill puts tension into the rig vertically.

The uphaul

The uphaul is used to pull the sail up and out of the water so that you can get under way. One end is connected to the boom end, while the other is allowed to dangle free – connected to the base of the mast by a short piece of elasticated shock-cord. This allows you to find the uphaul when the rig is lying in the water and then get enough leverage on the rig without having excessive lengths of rope dangling around your feet when you are sailing along.

The best uphaul for a beginner is the type that consists of a number of loosely intertwined lengths of rope. This is easy to grip anywhere along its length and you will not be limited to the three or four knots found on older style uphauls. Hawaiian uphauls should be avoided as these have no knots at all and are elasticated inside. Although they fit snugly to the mast, they are difficult to use.

Below: booms and boom ends come in a variety of shapes and sizes. Make sure your boom is the correct length and width for your sail.

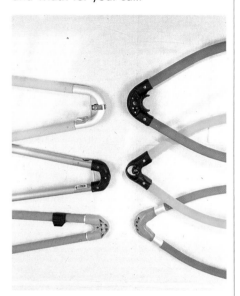

Above: some booms can be adjusted telescopically (top) or with the use of extension pieces (bottom).

Clothing and Accessories

Wetsuits

Some form of protective clothing is essential if you sail in a cold climate. Hypothermia, a medical condition in which the body's core temperature drops below the normal 98.6°F (37°C), is a real danger and can lead to uncontrolled shivering, disorientation and eventual death. (See section on safety). Wetsuits can insulate your body against the dangers of low temperatures and even in warmer climes they will make life more comfortable on cool windy days.

Wetsuits are made of a closed cell foam rubber called neoprene and work by trapping and insulating a thin layer of water against your skin. The water is then warmed by your own body heat. The neoprene is normally double-lined with nylon – once on the inside for comfort and once on the outside both for durability (raw 'smoothskin' snags easily) and for fashion considerations: plain neoprene is always black.

The degree of insulation against the cold offered by a wetsuit depends on the thickness of the neoprene. A lightweight summer suit would be around 2–3mm thick while a warmer winter suit could be up to 5–6mm thick. The disadvantage of thick neoprene is that it lacks flexibility, 5mm being about the thickest any energetic boardsailer could put up with.

There are other ways of increasing a suit's insulation properties, however. Steamers, the name given to one-piece winter suits, work on the principle that if water circulation in and out of the suit and round the body can be kept to a minimum, then the neoprene needn't be as thick as it would otherwise have to be. The seams on steamers are therefore glued and blindstitched (a process that doesn't pierce the neoprene from one side to the other), so that water cannot seep in or out. The neck, wrists and ankles are usually tight and the ankles often have straps that can be pulled taut to prevent water entering or escaping.

The efficiency of a wetsuit can also be enhanced by the use of 'smoothskin' instead of a double-lined neoprene. Smoothskin reduces heat loss by evaporation as water quickly runs off its smooth shiny surface.

Apart from one-piece steamers, wetsuits come in a variety of styles: shorties for warmer weather and long-john trouser and bolero-jacket combinations for all-round use (the jacket can be removed in warm weather). Whichever suit you chose, make sure it allows you sufficient

freedom of movement, especially in the arms. Manufacturers can influence the amount of flexibility in a suit by altering the cut and with the judicious use of thinner material in certain areas, such as under the arms. Beginners should avoid smoothskin, which is prone to damage by excessive wear, and look for suits with extra padding on the knees.

Drysuits

Traditional loose-fitting drysuits are made of a waterproof material – usually PVC-coated nylon or Goretex – and incorporate waterproof latex-rubber seals on the neck, wrists and ankles. Entry is usually through a heavy-duty waterproof zip across the back. However, they have no inbuilt insulation properties, so warm clothing must be worn underneath.

Top: wetsuits and drysuits. (From left to right) A traditional loose-fitting drysuit with latex seals and a back-entry zip; a double-lined long john wetsuit with a separate bolero top for all-round use; a thin shortie wetsuit for warmer weather and extra manoeuvrability; a close-fitting smoothskin drysuit with latex seals and a back-entry zip; and a one-piece steamer with sealed seams and tight wrists and ankles.

Above: harnesses. A harness designed for maximum manoeuvrability (top); a standard harness with a detachable buoyancy pad (left) and a harness with a large back pack for flares and spare line (right).

Above left: The correct way to load a roofrack.

Above: A board trolley can make a long walk to the water's edge more manageable.

Left: Just some of the many spares and accessories available from a windsurfing shop.

Although potentially very warm, this type of suit has its disadvantages: it's bulky and hardly flattering, the zip restricts movement and is hard to operate and somehow water nearly always gets into the suit – usually through the seals.

Some modern close-fitting drysuits are made of neoprene and are similar to one-piece wetsuits except that they have waterproof zips and latex seals. (Some two-piece versions have a form of rolled waist seal.) Although neoprene drysuits are also prone to leakage through the seals, they do have better insulation properties, they allow greater freedom of movement than traditional drysuits and they won't fill with water when torn.

Clothing accessories

Gloves, mitts, boots, neoprene socks and various forms of headgear are available to keep the cold-weather sailor a bit warmer. As the head is the area of maximum heat loss, suitable headgear is essential in very cold weather. Boots, or simple plastic shoes, have other advantages. They protect the feet against injury on the board, they make it easier to operate the daggerboard and they provide extra grip on the deck.

Harnesses

In all but the lightest winds, wearing a harness is essential if you intend to sail for any length of time. A harness hooks onto a line hanging down from the boom and relieves the strain on your arms. Although harnesses incorporate a small amount of buoyancy, they shouldn't be looked upon as life jackets as they will not support you face up in the water if you are knocked unconscious.

Harnesses come in many designs: small ones intended to allow maximum freedom of movement, bulky ones for extra buoyancy and easier water starting and low-slung models for added back support.

Roofracks

One of the joys of windsurfing is that your board is easily transportable on top of your car. However, having a secure roofrack and loading it correctly is important. Most roofrack manufacturers specify maximum load-carrying cap-acities, so don't exceed these. If you do carry more than one board, load one on top of the other. Tests have shown that the lift generated by two boards side by side is over double that of two boards stacked vertically on the roofrack. At high speeds this can seriously affect the straight line handling and cornering ability of your car and put excessive pressure on the front bar of your roofrack.

Strap your equipment on the rack securely and, if possible, use special mast clamps to prevent the mast slipping out of the straps as you are going along. Replace the straps themselves if they are frayed in any way.

Other accessories

The list of spares and accessories available in any windsurfing shop is almost endless and you will probably need most of them at one time or another during your windsurfing career. The list includes sail numbers for racing, roofracks and board trolleys for transporting your board, mast pads and boom bumpers for the protection of custom boards against damage from the rig, DIY repair kits and Mylar tape for mending minor damage to boards and sails, plus spare battens, footstraps, UJs, harness lines, flares, sail bags and, of course, kit bags in which to put everything!

Sailing Theory

The theory behind windsurfing may seem complex at first, but a basic understanding of the principles of sailing will not only make your first faltering attempts on a board a little less frustrating, it will also help you to progress through your windsurfing career at a much greater speed.

Sailing terms

Windsurfing has borrowed much of the terminology used in conventional sailing and has invented a bit of its own jargon. Most of the common terms are explained in the glossary at the end of this book but it is worthwhile explaining a few terms in detail here.

Apart from *port* and *starboard* (left and right respectively when looking towards the *front* of the board) and the names for the different pieces of equipment, most windsurfing terms relate in some way to the direction of the wind. Because the wind can only blow from one direction at a time, any object closer to the source of the wind is said to be to *windward* (i.e. upwind) and any object further away from the source of the wind is said to be to *leeward* (i.e. downwind).

Heading up means steering toward the source of the wind, i.e. to windward, while *bearing off* (or *bearing away*) means steering away from the source of the wind, i.e. to leeward. All of the points of sailing relate to the direction of the wind (see opposite), as do the terms for each of the two turning manoeuvres. A *tack* involves turning the nose of the board through the eye of the wind (i.e. turning to windward by up to 180 degrees) while a *gybe* involves turning the tail of the board through the eye of the wind (i.e. turning the board to leeward by up to 180 degrees).

A board can be said to be sailing on either a *port tack* or a *starboard tack*. On a port tack the wind will be blowing over the port side of the board, while on a

Unlike a conventional sailing craft, which heels to leeward as the wind increases, the rig on a sailboard must be raked over to windward while the board itself remains flat.

starboard tack the wind will be blowing over the starboard side. An easy way to determine which tack you are on is to look at your hands on the boom. Assuming you are in the normal sailing position, if your left (port) hand is closest to the mast you will be on a port tack but if your right (starboard) hand is closest to the mast then you will be on a starboard tack.

When controlling the amount of wind in the sail, the term *sheeting in* describes the action of pulling in the sail so that it fills with air. *Sheeting out* describes the action of letting the sail out so that the power in the sail is reduced. If the sail is let out too far, or the board heads into the wind too

much, then the sail will *luff*, or flutter, in the wind.

Although it is important to be familiar with most, if not all, windsurfing terms, too much jargon all at once only serves to confuse the mind of the beginner. If you don't understand the terms and principles in this section immediately, don't despair. Come back to them once you have experienced some of the fundamentals of windsurfing in practice and they will be much more understandable.

The principles of steering

As explained on page 19, the sail acts rather like a wing. As the wind flows over its curved surface, the pressure is reduced on the leeward side and the sail is sucked along. Or, in the case of running before the wind, the sail resists the force of the wind and is pushed along. The sum of all the forces acting on the sail can be imagined to act on one point only. This is known as the *centre of effort* (CE).

The effort in the sail would simply push the board sideways if it wasn't for the resistance offered by the daggerboard (and to a lesser extent the fin and any submerged parts of the hull). The daggerboard represents the *centre of lateral resistance* (CLR).

When the two forces are in equilibrium, that is, when the CE is directly above the CLR, the board will move in a straight line (see diagram). This phenomenon also explains how the board is steered. If the sail, and therefore the CE, is moved forward towards the nose of the board so that it is in front of the CLR, then the nose of the board will be pushed away from the wind. Conversely, if the CE is moved back towards the tail of the board and behind the CLR then the tail will be pushed away from the wind. The board pivots on the daggerboard, behaving rather like a revolving door. When either the nose or the tail is pushed away from the wind, the other end of the board will swing towards the wind.

Steering, therefore, involves tilting the sail forwards or backwards as necessary. When you are running with the wind, the sail will be at right angles to the board. Tilting the sail to port will make the nose of the board swing to starboard, and vice-versa.

Although steering a course is largely a matter of heading the board in the required direction, there are other influences in addition to the relative positions of the CE and CLR. Water conditions (waves, tides and currents) can affect the actual course sailed. Also, because the board never totally resists the sideways force of the sail, there will always be a degree of drift to leeward or *leeway*.

There is another form of steering which

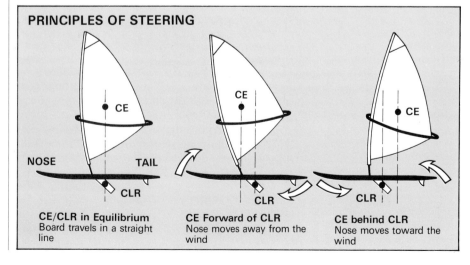

PRINCIPLES OF STEERING

NOSE · CE · **TAIL** · CLR

CE/CLR in Equilibrium
Board travels in a straight line

CE · CLR

CE Forward of CLR
Nose moves away from the wind

CE · CLR

CE behind CLR
Nose moves toward the wind

only comes into play at higher speeds when the board is planing. By forcing one edge of the board down into the water, extra drag is produced on that side and the board will turn in that direction. The board is effectively banked into the turn while the sail is left in a relatively neutral position. This is known as *footsteering*.

Points of sailing

A sailboard can sail in any direction except directly into the wind, and up to 45 degrees either side of it (see diagram). Within these limits the sail cannot be trimmed correctly and will luff. However, it is possible to sail a course towards a point directly upwind. This is achieved by *beating* – sailing a zig-zag course towards your final goal.

All points (directions) of sailing have names. *Reaching* refers to sailing across the wind. It is the fastest point of sailing and is normally qualified as a *broad reach*, a *beam reach* or a *close reach*. Sailing *close hauled* refers to sailing upwind as 'close' to the wind as possible (i.e. on a beating course) and *running* refers to sailing downwind.

Sail trim and apparent wind

Because the drive in the sail relies on the smooth flow of air over its surface, there is an optimum angle at which the sail should be held to the wind. The *chord line* of a sail is an imaginary line drawn from the mast to the clew of the sail (see diagram). If this chord line is at approximately 20 degrees to the wind, the sail will be correctly trimmed. If the angle of attack is too small and the sail is undertrimmed (sheeted out), the smooth air flow over the sail will break down and the sail will luff as the wind blows the sail back in on itself. If the angle of attack is too great and the sail is overtrimmed (sheeted in too much) the airflow on the leeward side will become very turbulent, reducing the drive in the sail. Of course, the wind is invisible and measuring the angle of attack impossible, so correctly

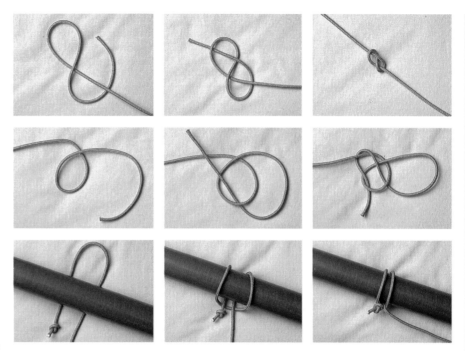

Some Useful Knots

Figure eight knot (Top row): Used to put a lump in a line to prevent it running through a cleat or another knot.

Bowline (Middle row): A slip-proof loop knot used on the downhaul and the outhaul.

Inhaul lashing (Bottom row): Used to tie the inhaul to the mast. (Some modern mast-to-boom connections do not require an inhaul lashing and work by wrapping the inhaul around the mast and through the boom end before the boom is moved to a position perpendicular to the mast. This applies tension to the inhaul itself and secures the connection.)

trimming the sail is a matter of 'feel' and experience.

So far it has been assumed that the wind blows from one direction only. From the sailor's point of view this is not so. If a sailboard were propelled through completely still air, not by wind but by some other means, it would still experience an effective wind created by its own motion. This wind, added to the 'true' wind experienced by someone standing still, produces the *apparent* wind. The sailor must therefore trim his sail according to the apparent wind rather than the true wind.

The faster the board is moving, the more the apparent wind will swing around to come from the direction in which the board is travelling. This is why boards moving fast on a broad reach will still have their sails trimmed in tightly. During gusts, the sail should be sheeted out as the apparent wind moves closer to the true wind and then sheeted in again to maintain trim.

POINTS OF SAILING

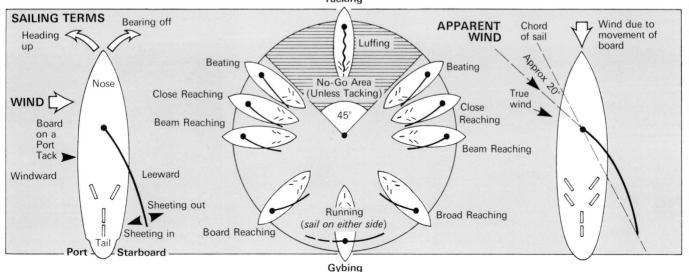

WINDSURFING IN PRACTICE

Rigging your board

Before attempting to sail, you will have to assemble the board and rig. Many people underestimate the importance of rigging the board properly; a loose mast-to-boom connection, a badly set sail or an uphaul that isn't attached to the mast foot can each make life difficult on the water.

The rigging procedure for all boards is fairly standard, with only minor differences between brands, and the instructions supplied with a new board should outline any special features it may have. With experience, you will be able to work out the routine for any board.

The basic procedure is as follows:

1 Slide the mast into the luff sleeve and then slide the mast extension (or mast foot) into the base of the mast, making sure it is clean of sand and grit.

2 Tension the downhaul. The downhaul connects the tack (bottom corner) of the sail to the mast foot and puts tension in the luff area of the sail. On systems without a pulley, tie a bowline in the line and then loop it twice through the eyelet on the sail before tying it off.

3 Attach the boom to the mast so that the uphaul line hangs down and the inhaul cleat (if any) is on top. Although most systems use an inhaul line, the exact lashing and cleating arrangements depend on the brand. Some require the inhaul to be lashed to the mast (see the knot on page 25) before it is passed through the holes on the boom end and then secured using a cleat. Others (such as that in the photos) simply require the inhaul to be wrapped around the boom end and the mast while the boom is at an acute angle to the mast. When the boom is swung around to sit at right angles to the mast, the inhaul line will be taut and the boom held tightly against the mast.

Above: before assembling the board and rig, check that you have all the necessary equipment (including a rig safety leash and a spare length of rope) and ensure that it is in good working order. Equipment failure at sea can be dangerous.

1. Slide the mast into the luff sleeve (tapered end first) and ensure the tip fits snugly into the cap at the head of the sail.

5. Secure the inhaul to the cleat on the boom and tie it off.

6. Swing the mast down until it is at right angles to the mast and tension is taken up by the inhaul.

Far left: A correctly rigged sail.

Above left and above: Two ways of carrying a board.

Bottom left: When carrying the rig, hold the boom and mast with each hand and keep the mast at right angles to the wind. This will prevent the wind from catching the sail and make it easier to handle.

4 Tension the outhaul. Some outhaul systems incorporate pulleys and some don't. If you have an adjustable boom, adjust it to fit the sail.

5 Insert the battens and secure them, using the 'lip' on the leech of the sail. Elastic cups at the far end of the batten pockets will keep the battens under tension. Some sails have buckles or Velcro straps to adjust tension.

6 Adjust the downhaul and outhaul. In order to set the sail without wrinkles or creases, it may be necessary to fine-tune it with the downhaul and outhaul. If the creases run horizontally from the luff to the clew, tighten the downhaul or loosen the outhaul. If the creases are vertical, loosen the downhaul or tighten the outhaul. If there are creases around the battens, adjust the batten tension. It may be impossible to set a sail perfectly with a mast that is either too stiff or too flexible, or with a sail that is stretched.

With experience, you will be able to give it either a flat setting for less power in stronger winds, or a full setting for more power in lighter winds.

7 Don't forget the uphaul. One end is normally left fastened to the boom at all times, but be sure to attach the other end to the mast foot with a piece of shock-cord. This will make it much easier to find when the rig is lying in the water.

2. Insert the mast extension (with the universal joint attached) into the base of the mast and tension the downhaul, using the cleat to secure it.

3. The boom should be attached somewhere between chin and eye level. Choose a position that is comfortable for you.

4. With the boom at an acute angle to the mast, wrap the inhaul line around the boom end.

7. Tension the outhaul (with your foot if necessary). A pulley system or line through the clew eyelet twice will give extra purchase.

8. Use the clew handle to hold tension in the sail while the outhaul line is fed through the cleat.

9. Slide the battens into the batten pockets. On fully battened sails, the battens should be inserted before the sail is tensioned.

Learning to sail

It is possible to sail a board on any stretch of water other than a fast-moving river. If you are learning, however, it is important that you try the board on flat water first. Ideally, the wind should be around a Force 2 to 3 (4 to 10 knots). More and you will be overpowered; less and you will drift around, unable to make the board react to your movements. The wind direction should be cross-shore, so that you can sail out and back at 90 degrees to the wind. Onshore winds will blow you back to the beach, while offshore winds, apart from being disturbed by obstacles on land and dangerously stronger the further you go out, will tend to blow you out to sea. If possible, choose a location with a 'lee shore' nearby, so that if you do get into trouble at least you will drift towards land. Take note of tides and currents. A strong tide can be dangerous. Inland waters, such as lakes and reservoirs are ideal. They are relatively flat; there are no tides or currents; and there is always a lee shore.

Using the correct equipment will make your first steps afloat much easier. The board should be long (at least 3.6 m or 12 ft) with a relatively flat underwater shape and plenty of volume to keep you afloat. Around 220 to 250 litres should suffice if you are of average weight. Avoid foot-straps; they will only get in the way. Make sure you are using a small sail, one with a short boom if possible. It will be easier to pull out of the water and it is always preferable to be underpowered rather than overpowered. Depending on your size and the strength of the wind, any 'marginal' sail 5 sq m (50 sq ft) or smaller will do.

Your main problem once on the water will be one of balance. Try to familiarize yourself with the feel of the board on the water by standing on it without the rig attached. Rock it from side to side and walk up and down its length. This will get you used to balancing the board while sailing and teach you where not to put your weight.

Your very first attempts to sail should be under the supervision of a qualified

Below: How the board reacts to movements of the sail. (Top row) From the stationary position (centre) inclining the rig forwards will swing the nose away from the wind (left). Inclining the rig back towards the tail will bring the nose up into the wind (right). (Bottom row) The same principle is used while under way. Incline the rig forwards to steer away from the wind (left), and backwards to head up towards the wind (right).

instructor. He or she will be able to explain the principles of sailing and point out any mistakes you are making. More importantly perhaps, he will also ensure that you are familiar with the safety aspects of windsurfing and that you are able to 'self-rescue' (See pages 86–89).

A proper windsurfing school will have some form of classroom facilities (even if it's just a blackboard on the beach) so that the instructor can illustrate the theory of sailing, and it should have a dry-land simulator. This is a board (or part of a board) mounted on a swivelling turntable. The board doesn't go anywhere; it just swivels round depending on which way you move the rig – in exactly the same way as a real board behaves on the water. The only difference is that you don't get wet when you fall off!

Once you have experienced sailing on dry land, the instructor will take you through your first steps on the water: uphauling the rig, rotating the board and the rig, getting under way, steering, turning and returning to your starting point.

A typical course can last anywhere between six hours and a whole weekend. The school normally provides equipment (with the exception of a wetsuit) and some will allow you to return free of charge on another day if conditions take a turn for the worse and you are unable to complete the course.

Be prepared to fall off a number of times during your first attempts at windsurfing. Don't worry – everyone does it and you should regard it as part of the fun of learning. It is worthwhile practising the basic movements of the sail on land before venturing out onto the water. With the correct procedure clear in your head, you can then concentrate on balancing on the board rather than wondering what to do next. The photographs on these pages illustrate how the board reacts to movements of the sail and the correct procedure for getting under way.

Uphauling

Put the rig in the water first and then attach it to the board in about approx 1 metre (3–4ft) of water. This prevents the daggerboard (which should be in its down position) from scraping on the bottom.

Position the board so that it is at right angles to the wind with the rig to leeward (downwind) and the clew pointing in the same direction as the back of the board. Climb on, keeping your weight over the centreline of the board. Grasp the uphaul, balancing your weight against it and position your feet either side of the mast foot. As you stand up, keep your back straight and raise the rig out of the water

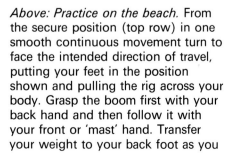

Above: Practice on the beach. From the secure position (top row) in one smooth continuous movement turn to face the intended direction of travel, putting your feet in the position shown and pulling the rig across your body. Grasp the boom first with your back hand and then follow it with your front or 'mast' hand. Transfer your weight to your back foot as you sheet in and the sail fills with wind. The final photograph shows the correct sailing position from another angle. The stronger the wind, the further you must lean out.

by pulling hand over hand on the uphaul. It may seem heavy at first, but it will get lighter as you pull it out. Beware of falling in backwards.

Grasp the mast with your front hand (the one nearest the nose of the board) and hold the rig so that it is at 90 degrees to the board with the sail flapping freely in the wind. This is called the 'mast abeam' or 'secure' position.

There will be occasions (after you fall in backwards, for example) when either the board, the rig or both will be out of position. There are three possibilities: (a) the board is pointing in the wrong direction, (b) the rig is lying to windward (i.e. between you and the wind), (c) a combination of the first two.

As you will have read in the section on sailing theory (page 24), the board behaves like a revolving door, pivoting

around the daggerboard when the rig is inclined forwards or backwards. So, in order to point the board in the right direction, incline the rig towards the tail of the board. As the nose of the board heads up into the wind, continue to incline the rig in the same direction and shuffle around the front of the board until it is on the correct heading. The amount of incline governs the speed at which the board will pivot so take it easy and concentrate on maintaining your balance until you can return to the secure position.

Opposite top: Rotating the board. Uphaul the rig until it is clear of the water and then incline it towards the tail of the board. Continue to incline it in that direction as you shuffle the board around onto its new heading.

Opposite bottom: The windward uphaul. As the rig breaks free of the water, swing it around the nose or the tail of the board. Balance your weight against it and use your feet to keep the board on the same heading.

If the rig is lying to windward, begin the uphauling procedure as normal, but as the rig comes out of the water, swing it round either the nose or tail of the board (whichever suits you), using your feet to keep the board on the same heading. The stronger the wind, the more it will want to swing by itself, so lean back and balance your weight against it. Stop swinging when you are able to regain the secure position. If both the board and rig are out of position, return the rig to leeward before pivoting the board round.

Getting under way

Once you are comfortably positioned with your back to the wind and the rig at 90 degrees to the board (the secure position), you are ready to start sailing.

Turn to face the nose of the board and the intended direction of travel, making sure that your way ahead is clear. Move your feet back, letting your front foot point towards the nose of the board. As you do this, pull the rig across the front of your body until it balances on the mast foot and becomes quite light. Put your back hand on the boom and follow it with your 'mast hand'.

You are now in a position to sheet in (pull with your back hand). As the sail fills with wind, transfer your weight to your back foot in order to counteract the pull of the sail. If there is too much pull, sheet out a little. By deftly shifting your weight from one foot to the other and by sheeting in and out as necessary, you will remain balanced and sailing in a straight line.

Sometimes, in the early stages of getting under way, the board has a tendency to head up into the wind. If this happens, incline the rig towards the nose, but don't sheet out. The board will then start to move as the nose turns away from the wind.

Below: Getting under way. Uphaul the rig and hold the mast in the secure position. Turn to face forward, pulling the rig across your body. Transfer your hands to the boom (back hand first) and sheet in. To prevent the board heading up into the wind, rake the rig forwards slightly as if you were trying to point to the nose of the board with the mast.

Sailing a course, tacking and gybing

Once under way and sailing in a straight line, it is important to trim and re-trim the sail in order to deal with gusts of wind or any alterations in the wind's direction. Changes in wind direction – due to obstacles on shore, for example – can be dealt with by sheeting in or out to re-trim the sail, or by altering course. Gusts, however, can cause real problems for inexperienced sailors. The sudden increase of power in the sail is often too much to deal with and can frequently result in a catapult fall – the rig picks up the sailor and literally flings him over the nose of the board.

You can recognize a gust approaching by looking for the tell-tale ripples on the surface of the water. When it hits, be prepared to sheet out and, if the gust is too strong, to lean back against the increased pull of the sail.

Correct stance is important. Never assume what is known as the toilet position – backside sticking out, back at right angles to the legs, knees bent. Try and keep your hips and backside in and your back straight and upright instead. This enables you to lean back and sheet out at the same time during a gust. The ungainly toilet position leaves you with no option but to be pulled in by the rig.

With an upright stance you will also find it easier to deal with lulls. As the wind dies, you will be able to get your weight back over the board quickly and easily before you fall in backwards.

When learning, it is a good idea to establish a goal point towards which you can sail at 90 degrees to the wind (sailing across the wind). Any stationary object such as a buoy, a moored boat, or even a tree on an opposite shore will do. If the board then strays off course, you will be able to steer it back onto the correct heading using the goal point as a guide.

A sailboard is steered by altering the position of the sail, which in effect means altering the position of the centre of effort (CE) in the sail in relation to the centre of lateral resistance (CLR) in the hull.

As illustrated on page 24, tilting the CE forward of the CLR makes the board bear away, i.e. turn away from the wind, while bringing the CE behind the CLR makes the board head up into the wind. In practice, this means swinging the rig forward and slightly to windward by extending your front arm when you want to bear off, and extending your back arm to draw the rig back across your body when you want to head up (see the photos on page 28).

An easy way to remember which steering method to use is to imagine what happens to the clew (the far end of the boom). Bring the clew up to turn away from the wind; let the clew fall to turn towards the wind.

Once the board has been returned to the correct heading, you can maintain a straight course by keeping the CE and CLR in equilibrium. As the CLR is normally situated in the daggerboard in a light wind and the CE roughly in the centre of the sail, this means that the rig is held in an upright position.

In a heavier wind, when the board begins to plane and only its rear section is in the water, the CLR will move back and so the rig must be raked further back in order to maintain equilibrium and a straight course.

Turning

There are only two ways of turning a sailboard around. You can either bring the nose through the eye of the wind (a tack) or you can bring the tail through the eye of the wind (a gybe). Which manoeuvre you choose to use will depend on the direction in which you are sailing.

Tacking, as the turn that is made into the wind, is a useful manoeuvre when you are trying to gain ground upwind. The word tacking is also used to describe a zig-zag course sailed upwind. It is impossible to sail directly into the wind, but by sailing on a diagonal course across the wind at about 45 degrees to it, tacking, and then sailing on the opposite diagonal, it is possible to arrive at a destination directly upwind of your starting point.

Gybing is the opposite of tacking and is primarily used when sailing off the wind (i.e. at an angle greater than 90 degrees to the wind) and losing ground downwind is not important. Because you are travelling downwind and it is possible to keep power in the sail for a lot longer than during a tack, gybing has become the favourite manoeuvre of more advanced sailors over recent years and there are now many different forms of it.

These and the more advanced forms of tacking are covered in the next two sections. This section concentrates on basic tacking and gybing techniques. It is important to practise these manoeuvres until you can perform them smoothly and easily. Good basic technique will bring endless benefits when you move onto more advanced forms of windsurfing.

Tacking

The basic principles of tacking are simple: head the board up into the wind and, as the board's nose passes through the eye of the wind, step around the mast so that you can grasp the boom on the other side of the sail before sheeting in and sailing away on the opposite tack.

A problem many beginners experience is that they can't maintain the momentum of the board throughout the turn. When the board is steered into the wind, it simply comes comes to a halt. So, rather than attempt to to turn around in a smooth arc in the early stages of learning how to tack, it is often a better idea to simply stop, turn on the spot and start again as normal. This is known as the 'rope tack'.

In practice there is very little difference between the rope tack and the technique for rotating the board described on page 30. When you want to turn, sheet out, take a step forward and put your feet either side of the mast, taking hold of the

uphaul rope as you do so. Keep your back to the wind and incline the rig towards the tail of the board until the nose swings around to point on its new heading. Shuffle around the mast as the board turns and try to keep the clew out of the water. Start again in the normal manner by drawing the rig back across your body, moving your feet back, transferring your hands to the boom and sheeting in.

Having mastered the rope tack you can then learn the proper tack in stages. Start by holding the mast rather than the uphaul during the turn and then try steering the board into the turn by raking the rig back as if you were trying to dip the clew end of the boom in the water, near the tail of the board. As the board comes round into the wind you will have to trim the sail by sheeting right in. You can help the turn by keeping your weight back on the board (near the leeward rail if possible) before the board heads into the wind and you are forced to move around the mast. If the board comes to a stop during the turn, help it around the rest of the way by inclining the rig back as in the basic rope tack.

When you become more confident, you will be able to keep the rig raked back until it is over the centreline of the board. You can then move quickly around the mast as the board passes through the wind, swapping your hands on the mast as you go. Throw the rig forward to help the board bear off, then move your weight back, sheet in and sail off on your new course.

Below right to left:

The beginner's tack. Make sure your turning area is clear.

Rake the rig back so that the board heads up into the wind. Step forward and put one hand on the mast.

If the board doesn't pass through the eye of the wind before it comes to a halt, stand with your back to the wind and incline the rig towards the tail of the board.

The board will turn through the eye of the wind as you shuffle around the mast. Continue to incline the rig in the same direction.

Bottom row: When the board is on its new heading, assume the secure position.

Transfer your hand to the boom.

Lean back slightly, sheet in and sail off on the new tack.

33

Gybing

As opposed to a tack, in which you must move your body to the other side of the sail, during a gybe your body stays put and the rig is swung around the front of the board. The gybe is really the exact opposite of the tack: you bear off downwind until the tail of the board passes through the eye of the wind and then 'flip' the rig around.

As with the tack, it is easier to start off with a very simplified version of the turn – the rope gybe. As with the rope tack, this involves sailing across the wind, stopping, rotating the board and then starting again on the new heading. The only difference is that the board is rotated in the opposite direction.

The rope gybe is one of the simplest windsurfing manoeuvres and it shouldn't take long to master. Start by bearing off a little and then sheeting out so that the board slows to a halt. Hold the uphaul rope (or the mast if you prefer) and release your back hand from the boom. Transfer this hand to the uphaul and release your other hand, which can now be used to help you keep your balance. Now, swing the rig towards the nose of the board,

keeping your back to the wind, and help the board to rotate by using your feet.

As the boom swings around within reach, you can use your free hand to pull it around the rest of the way. (Beware of doing this too quickly and pulling the leech of the sail through the eye the wind, as this will knock you off the board.) Pulling the rig around with your free hand will put you in the right position to sheet in and get the board under way on its new heading.

The more you practise this manoeuvre, the earlier you will be able to grab the opposite boom and pull it around. (In fact, the sail fills with air and stays roughly where it is, while the board rotates beneath your feet.) This is called a 'power gybe', although it is not be confused with the carve gybe which is described on page 62. You can help the board to turn during this sort of gybe by putting some weight on the windward or outside rail, i.e. the rail opposite the direction in which the board is turning.

Having mastered the simple rope and power gybes, you can move on to the standard gybe. The main difficulty encountered by most novice sailors is

Below (Clockwise bottom to top): The beginner's gybe. **From your normal sailing position, sheet out.**

Hold the uphaul rope (or the mast) and take a step forward.

Change your hands on the uphaul and start to swing the rig around.

Continue to sweep the rig around, pushing the board in the opposite direction with your foot.

Use your free hand to pull on the opposite boom as the rig comes around.

Return your feet to the normal sailing position, pull the rig across your body, sheet in and go.

getting the board to bear off sufficiently far downwind so that the rig can be flipped around. The correct technique is as follows: bear off onto a broad reach by tilting the rig forward but keeping the sail sheeted in (quite tightly in a light wind). Help the board to turn by putting weight on the windward or outside rail. As the wind swings around behind you, square off the rig (i.e. sheet out) and move your feet so that they are astride the centreline of the board and slightly behind the daggerboard case.

You will now be starting to sail directly downwind on a run, so lean the mast out towards what was the windward side of the board. You may even have to move your hands back down the boom to get the rig far enough over. Keep the whole rig tilted back over your head as well. This aids control and will help to prevent the sail from pulling you over the front of the board.

Try and keep your weight over the board. You can do this by keeping the bottom half of your body upright with your hips over the board, while your upper body is leant sideways to push the mast to windward. Bending your leeward

knee will help you to put your weight on the windward rail with your other leg without falling in sideways.

There are two methods of flipping the rig around the nose of the board and each uses different hand positions:
a) Move your front (mast) hand to the mast itself and then let go of the boom with your back hand. Allow the rig to swing around (the board will continue to turn) and then put your free hand on the boom so that it becomes your new front hand while you release your other hand from the mast. Pull the rig across your body, grip the boom with your new back hand and sheet in.
b) This method is more sophisticated but is useful to learn as it is used in the more advanced forms of gybing. With the rig tilted back, release your back hand first so that the rig swings around. Use your old back hand to hold the mast and then release the hand still on the boom and use it to grip the boom on the other side. Pull the rig across the front of your body, resume the normal sailing position, sheet in and sail off. It is relatively easy to get under way again as you will already be on a broad or beam reach after the gybe.

Above (Clockwise bottom to top):
The gybe. Bear off onto a broad reach, stand astride the centreline of the board and keep the rig back.

As the board heads downwind, sheet out and push the mast to windward.

Help the board around by putting weight on your windward foot.

When the tail passes through the eye of the wind, release your back hand and place it on the mast.

As the rig flips around, move your front hand from the boom and place it on the opposite side.

Pull the rig across your body, sheet in and continue to sail.

Points of sailing

As your sailing technique becomes more refined, you will begin to notice the differences between the alternative points of sailing. Initially, you will probably stick to sailing at 90 degrees to the wind (a beam reach), but as you become more competent you can practise sailing on an upwind course and on a downwind course. Each of these points of sailing requires a different technique.

Beating involves sailing upwind as close to the wind as possible. To sail on a beat you must sail closehauled, i.e. with the sail trimmed very tightly against your body and with the board 'pointing' as high as it will go.

It can be very tricky judging whether you are travelling upwind as close to the wind as you can as there is a fine line between sailing too low, and therefore losing ground to windward, and sailing too high and continually luffing the sail. The only way to ensure that you are pointing as high as possible is to head up slightly, but as soon as the sail shows any sign of luffing, bear off a bit.

The course steered is not necessarily the course sailed, for there will always be a bit of leeway. You should always have the daggerboard fully down when beating as it provides lateral resistance and prevents the board slipping sideways.

There is a particular stance for beating which you should adopt as soon as you are able: keep your hands quite close together on the boom and either side of the point of maximum draught on the sail; keep your feet close together with your front foot facing forward and lean your hips towards the front of the board. This puts your weight on the mast foot (via the boom) and keeps the full length of the board in the water, helping the daggerboard to resist leeway and preventing the tail from digging in and producing unwanted drag. If you have a mast track, move it forward, and if you are sailing in a stronger wind, keep your feet near the windward rail to prevent the daggerboard hydroplaning or 'railing'.

The beat is not the easiest or most enjoyable point of sailing, but you will often find yourself downwind of your starting point and being able to beat efficiently will get you upwind that much more quickly.

Reaching describes sailing directly across the wind and is the fastest point of sailing. Sailing at 90 degrees to the wind is called a 'beam reach'; slightly upwind of a beam reach is a 'close' or 'fine reach'; and downwind of a beam reach is a 'broad reach'.

As with all points of sailing, it is important to trim the sail correctly on a reach. You will know if the sail is undertrimmed when it starts to luff, but an overtrimmed sail is more difficult to recognize. When the airflow starts to break down on the leeward side of the sail there will still be plenty of pull in the sail, but it will not be contributing to forward drive – merely pulling you over to leeward. To trim the sail correctly, sheet out until the sail is on the verge of luffing and then sheet in slightly.

Above left: Sailing closehauled. Note how the sail is trimmed close to the body.

Above: A beam reach.

Far left: A broad reach.

Left: A run. Note how the rig is held at right angles to the board.

The faster you go, the more the sail needs to be sheeted in. This is because the apparent wind swings round to blow at a more acute angle to the direction of travel. This is why the sail trim for a fast broad reach is similar to a slower close reach.

Because there is less lateral resistance required on a reach, especially a broad reach, it is possible then to retract the daggerboard. This will allow the board to move faster and prevents the daggerboard itself from hydroplaning. The degree to which the daggerboard can be retracted depends on the exact point of sailing and on your speed.

When sailing on a reach in light winds, keep your weight forward on the board. This prevents the tail from sinking and keeps the rig upright and more powerful. As the wind increases you can lean back against the pull of the sail (allowing it to hold you up) and move your feet back down the board, raking the rig back as

you go. Initially, you may have to have your legs spread quite far apart, bending your back knee as the pull in the sail increases. This soon becomes impractical, however, and as your technique improves you should be able to keep your feet closer together. Don't move your feet back too quickly or the tail will sink, produce extra drag and prevent the board from accelerating.

Running directly downwind is considered to be the most difficult point of sailing. The biggest problem on a run is one of stability, but preventing the board from rocking from side to side is really a matter of experience. Some funboards are so unstable on a run that it is a better idea to sail a series of broad reaches downwind rather than endure a difficult and uncomfortable run.

The correct position for sailing on a run is to have your feet situated on either side of the centreline with with the rig at 90 degrees to the board. To give yourself

Stopping. If the pull of the sail becomes too much for you, or you simply want to avoid a collision, it is possible to stop in a very confined space: sheet out (backwinding the sail if necessary) and hold onto the mast while crouching down and laying the rig in the water. Crouching down allows you to keep your balance and the rig will be in the correct position for uphauling again if you so wish.

more control, crouch down and pull the rig over your head – the stronger the wind the further you should pull it back. This keeps your centre of gravity low and reduces the pull of the sail. Keeping the daggerboard down helps to stabilize the board in light winds but will make it oversteer in heavier winds, so it may be better to retract it.

FUNBOARDING

FUNBOARDING

Before modern funboards first began to appear in the early 1980s, the average boardsailor would pack up and go home when the wind passed the Force 4 mark (11–16 knots). Even if the sailor was able to control an increasingly unmanageable rig, he would have found it difficult to stay on a strapless board that bounced over the waves and out of control. What became known as the Force 4 barrier was a formidable obstacle to progress for the ambitious sailor.

The reasons were two-fold. Only a select few (most of them resident in Hawaii) had managed to master the correct methods of high-wind sailing, and these were the pioneers of modern funboard techniques. And, secondly, equipment available at the time was ill-designed for the quick response and ease of control necessary in strong winds. Standard sails, even those of the smaller 'storm' variety, would allow the centre of effort to wander wildly around during gusts, forcing the sailor to continually wrestle with the rig. Boards, which had big voluminous tails, would skip and bounce across the waves, eventually 'spinning out' and forcing the sailor to lose control, even if he had footstraps. Daggerboards, which were at best only pivotal and wouldn't retract completely, acted like hydrofoils, forcing their way to the surface and causing the board to tip over or 'rail'.

The first short boards – designed along the lines of surfboards – and their longer cousins, the first all-round funboards, revolutionized windsurfing. What had once been a barrier – winds over Force 4 – soon became a prerequisite for exciting sailing. Both techniques and equipment developed hand in hand, making life a lot easier for the modern boardsailor. Rigs are now much more stable so that a much larger and more powerful sail can be used in a given wind strength; footstraps are now standard on all but the very basic boards; nearly all daggerboards retract; and hull shapes have become much more sophisticated.

One of the most influential advances in strong-wind technique came when it was realized that, when a board is planing (i.e. travelling at high speed with minimal water displacement), its direction can be altered without the use of the rig. In other words, it could be 'footsteered' in much the same way as a surfboard or a waterski. Footsteering paved the way for many modern funboard techniques, including carve gybing and wave riding, and it resulted in today's designers paying a great deal more attention to the hydrodynamics of a board – especially underneath the hull and in the tail section.

A funboard is a board of any length that is designed to footsteer and perform at its best in winds of approximately Force 4 and above. Longer funboards have retractable daggerboards and adjustable mast tracks but all funboards have footstraps, and thin tails of one design or another. The term 'funboarding' itself now covers nearly every aspect of windsurfing except the beginner's stages (which are always carried out in light to medium winds). The more complex manoeuvres associated with sailing in strong winds – water starting, carve gybing and so on – are covered in the section on high-performance windsurfing (see page 52). The average sailor cannot hope to master these kinds of manoeuvres until he or she has had a minimum of a few months' experience on a long board in light to medium winds, a time that should be spent consolidating basic sailing techniques and perfecting the more advanced forms of intermediate sailing. This section, Funboarding or Intermediate Windsurfing, deals with all the aspects of board handling that every boardsailor has to master before taking on the challenging and exhilarating art of sailing in big waves and high winds.

Sailing a funboard in strong winds.

Beach Starting and Returning to Shore

Ironically, the roughest part of the sea is often exactly where you would prefer it to be at its flattest – just off the shore where the waves start to break as they meet the beach. Some shorebreaks are worse than others but all of them make uphauling difficult. The beach start was developed as a quick and easy way to launch, as it does away with the need to walk or swim your board past the breaking waves to the flatter water beyond, which on some beaches could be yards away.

By holding the rig with your front hand (the hand nearest the front of the board)

Beach starting

Below left: Place your front hand on the mast just above the boom and hold onto a footstrap with your back hand. If your board isn't fitted with straps, then hold onto it either by the tail, or angle the board and hold onto the skeg. The daggerboard should be retracted.

Below right: Head the board on a beam, or broad reach, and walk into the water (tilting the board if necessary) just after a wave breaks.

Bottom left: When the water is deep enough (knee height is about right), step onto the board with your back

foot. Don't put it too close to the tail or the board will sink and the skeg will hit the bottom. It is a matter of personal choice whether you move your front hand onto the boom before you step onto the board or whether you leave it on the mast for extra control.

Bottom right: Sheet in as you bring your forward foot up so that the board gets underway immediately. Beware of letting the board head up into the wind as you step aboard. This could cause the board to luff just as it should be picking up speed.

and the board with your back hand you simply walk into the water between two waves, step onto the board and sail off. Good timing is the essence of a good beach start. By carefully watching the waves you can launch on flat water between two waves and so avoid the worst consequences of the shorebreak. Waves come in 'sets' rather than in strictly regular intervals and with experience you will learn to recognize the longer gaps between waves and so increase your chances of launching successfully.

Ideally, you should launch in a cross-shore wind so that you can head directly out to sea on a reach with your daggerboard retracted completely. If you find yourself standing in the water with your board heading in the wrong direction (if it comes up into the wind, for example) it is easy to manoeuvre it into the right position by pushing down or pulling up on the boom. Because the daggerboard is retracted, the board will pivot around the skeg. Pushing down on the boom (and hence the mast foot) will push the nose of the board downwind; pulling up on the boom will bring the nose upwind. This is worth practising in shallow, calm water until you can do it automatically and without thinking.

Although the beach start is a considerably more convenient and graceful method of getting underway, it cannot be used in all situations. Direct onshore or offshore winds, for example, make beach starting a lot more difficult, although not necessarily impossible. Apart from the dubious wisdom of sailing in a directly offshore wind, you will be starting almost on a run and so your board will be at its most unstable. In a directly onshore wind you will have to approach the shorebreak at quite an angle in order to launch on a beat. Timing and speed are essential here; otherwise a wave will break over your board and more likely than not dump you back on the beach in a heap.

When the beach is steeply shelving or very rocky, or when the waves are particularly big, it would be a better idea to swim out past the break and start in the conventional manner. In this case try to keep the board between yourself and the shore on your way out (so that a wave doesn't dump it on top of you) and try to prevent a wave breaking onto your rig. Water is very heavy and can easily stretch and rip your sail, or even break your mast.

Landing and recovery

Returning to shore and recovering your board before ploughing nose first into the sand (or rocks!) is almost the reverse of a beach start. Again, timing is important as the idea is to land and recover between

Landing in surf

Top left: Aim to arrive at the shore break on the back of a breaking wave.

Top right: Having jumped off the board when the water is shallow enough, release your back hand and lift the board by a footstrap or the tail.

Above left: Walk the board up the beach until the nose is about to run aground.

Above right: Walk the tail of the board through the eye of the wind, letting the rig flip over as you do so, and pull the board out of the water.

Shorter and lighter boards, which tend to be more prone to damage on rocks and pebbles etc., can be lifted right out of the water instead.

two waves. However, whereas you can simply stand and wait before beach starting, when returning to shore you will have to judge your approach accurately as you will have only one chance to get it right.

Starting well ahead is a distinct advantage: sail towards the shore and when it's convenient 'feather' the sail in order to let a wave pass beneath you. It is then simply a matter of sheeting in to keep up with the wave (without overtaking it) and letting it break right in front of you. This will maximize the time available for stepping off and recovering your board before the next wave breaks.

The procedure for launching and recovering short boards is the same as it is for long boards. The only difference is that if the short board is light enough you will be able to carry it in and out of the water, so making the whole operation faster and more efficient, as you will be able to place the board with the wind in precisely the right direction when launching it.

The Harness

Once you feel confident in stronger winds (Force 3 or more), your first objective should be to master the sailboard harness. The harness allows you to use your body weight to counteract the force in the sail while at the same time relieving the strain on your arms. No matter how fit you are, sailing in strong winds would be either a painful or a short-lived affair without the aid of a harness.

Harnesses were first used at about the same time as the invention of footstraps and various systems were investigated at the time – including one devised by a German called Dorothy Burger, which employed moulded rubber gloves attached to the boom! The modern harness, which utilizes a chest hook and lines hanging from the boom, was developed by the Hawaiians as an adaptation of the trapeze harness used by catamaran sailors. Today this system is universal and indispensible for high-wind sailing, the only two significant improvements over the original being the use of a V-shaped safety hook and a spreader bar.

The safety hook, whether made of plastic or metal, will automatically release the harness line should it become tangled after a fall, and so allow you to escape from underneath the sail. As an additional precaution, some harnesses incorporate quick-release buckles just in case. Some manufacturers still use plain hooks on their harnesses – avoid them.

The spreader bar is an aid to comfort as it literally spreads the load so that your back, rather than your ribs, takes the

strain. On a harness without a spreader bar, the webbing material that connects the hook to the harness itself will compress your rib cage, and this becomes increasingly painful.

Using a harness

Having mastered the harness, you will wonder what the fuss was about because it really is simplicity itself. Your task will be a great deal easier if your harness lines are correctly positioned; the centre of each line should fall roughly in line with the centre of effort in the sail. Try positioning each line about shoulder-width apart on

the boom. Then, by holding the centre of each line, see which way the rig twists off. If it twists forward, move the lines forward and vice-versa. The actual length of each line will depend on a number of different factors – wind strength and boom height, for example, but personal preference should be the governing factor. Of course, this can only be established by trial and error. In theory, and sometimes in practice, if the lines are correctly positioned you should be able to hook in and sail with no hands on the boom.

Hooking in, as it is called, is what usually causes problems, especially in

Hooking in. Pull the boom towards you and bend your knees so that you hook in as you lower your chest – as in the photographs. If you prefer your hook facing up, hook in as you straighten up and lean back to take the weight of the rig. To unhook, pull the boom towards you and lift or drop your chest to let the line fall out.

strong winds. The trick is to pull the rig towards you with both arms – don't lean towards the rig because you will become unbalanced – at the same time bending your knees slightly. The harness line should then fall into place. Ease the rig back and slowly take the strain with your body, leaving your arms slightly bent to sheet in and out as normal.

Unhooking is simply the reverse. Pull the rig towards you and, if your hook is pointing up, bend your knees slightly. The line should then come free.

A final hint is to hook in while sailing close to the wind. Losing control on a fast reach will cause a spectacular, but potentially dangerous, catapult fall.

Left: using a harness. Note how the sailor's weight is taken by the harness lines and that her arms are slightly bent.

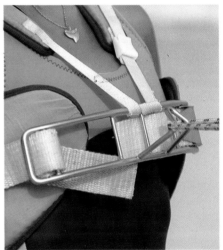

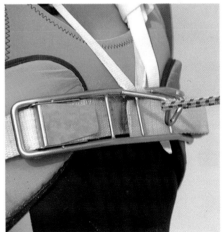

Whether you wear your hook up or down is a matter of personal choice.

Using an Adjustable Mast Track

The mast track is used to trim the board and, although originally developed so that the board could be finely tuned during a race, the track is now a recognized aid to recreational sailing.

By trimming the board you alter the plane on which it is travelling, i.e. you can choose to have a nose-high or a nose-down attitude. So, as the power of the sail is transferred to the board through both your body and the mast foot, having the mast at the rear of the track (and your feet a little further back) will give the board a nose-high attitude. This has a number of advantages:

a) If you are travelling at speed, then the planing area, and hence drag, will be reduced and your speed will be increased.

b) During fast turns a board pivots on its rear section. With a nose-high attitude the centre and forward rails won't 'grab' the water and prevent the board from turning.

c) Finally, if you are surfing down the face of a wave, however large or small it may be, a mast at the rear of the track will help to prevent the nose of the board from digging into the water or the wave ahead.

Having a nose-high attitude is not always beneficial, however. Unless the board is already planing it will mean that the tail is also digging into the water and preventing the board from accelerating. So, trimming the board by moving the mast forward in the track will help the board onto the plane, especially in marginal conditions. (Anyone who has ever driven a speed-boat will know that

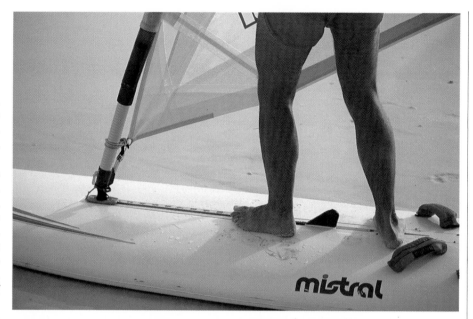

Mast-track positioning
As a rule of thumb, the mast should be forward in the track when you are sailing upwind or in marginal conditions, and in the rear position when you are fast reaching. A central or neutral position is a compromise between the two and should be used if you are in doubt or if you find adjusting the track difficult. Most mast tracks can be operated at sea with the use of a pedal-release system.

moving weight toward the bows will quickly encourage planing.)

Having a nose-down attitude with the mast forward in the track will also help the board to sail upwind. The complete length of the board will be in the water and a long waterline length (as it is called) produces extra lateral resistance and therefore improved upwind ability. Having the mast forward in the track also moves the centre of effort (CE) in the sail forward, reducing the risk of luffing when sailing to windward and allowing the sailor to use a larger sail than he otherwise would have been able to handle.

Mast tracks on long funboards are nearly always supplied with pedal-release systems and some will have spring-loaded devices to help the mast move in the track. Whether your track is spring-loaded or not, adjusting the mast at sea is easier if you use the boom as a lever. To help the mast move when pulling it back, press firmly down on the boom with your front hand and pull up with your back hand. Reverse the direction of pressure with each hand to move the mast forward.

Footstraps, retracting daggers and tracks may be too much to handle all at once if you are new to funboards. In that case, you can leave the mast in a neutral position with no real harm being done.

Rather than have adjustable mast tracks, most short boards have a 'fin-box' mast-track system using a moulded plastic box identical to that used to house the fin or skeg underneath the board. These should be set on shore according to the conditions on the day and your particular sailing style.

Using a Retractable Daggerboard

Sometimes, when sailing upwind, you never seem to reach the point you were aiming at, despite the fact that the board was heading towards it. This could be caused by a subtle shift of the wind but it could also be caused by insufficient lateral resistance. So the retractable dagger-board is used to provide lateral resistance when sailing upwind – it stops the board drifting sideways. In higher winds, or on short boards (below 3.2m – 10ft 4in) you will not need a dagger at all as the rails and the hull itself should provide all the necessary resistance.

Most daggerboards will allow you to adjust their fit in the slot – usually by means of a tensioned plastic screw – and will protrude above the deck in some way so that they can be adjusted by foot. You can raise and lower the dagger with either

foot, whichever is more comfortable or convenient. If possible, keep one foot in the footstrap if you are planing. Roll the daggerboard tip forward to raise it (or backwards to lower it) with the ball of your foot in one smooth movement.

Daggerboards have the annoying habit of hydroplaning and causing the board to 'rail up' and even capsize. Avoid this by lowering the dagger as far as you can before hydroplaning begins.

If you have problems adjusting the dagger while you are travelling upwind, try bearing off a little so that the lateral pressure on the daggerboard is reduced and it begins to adjust easily. For all offwind sailing the dagger should be retracted completely.

Daggerboard positioning.
The degree to which the daggerboard should be raised or lowered depends on a number of factors: the length of your board and the size of the dagger itself, the wind strength, and the direction in which you wish to go. Generally speaking, the dagger should be fully retracted for all offwind sailing, semi-retracted for close reaching, and fully extended for beating. This particular daggerboard arrangement has two protruding knobs – one for raising and one for lowering the dagger. However, most daggerboards have only one knob.

Fast Tacking

Tacking is frequently described as the least favoured manoeuvre in the funboard sailor's repertoire. Funboards are primarily designed for gybing and tend to have less volume in their forward sections – with a consequent reduction in stability when tacking. Tacking also involves heading up into the wind and this usually means that the board will come off the plane, and even, on occasions, stop.

However, tacking is often necessary, whether it is because you need to sail upwind to return to your launching point, because you are taking part in course racing or simply because you have to avoid an obstacle.

The beginner's only objective when learning to tack is to turn the board round without falling off. On the other hand, the funboard sailor should be able to tack quickly and efficiently. His objectives should be to get the sail on the opposite tack with the minimum of fuss and gain as

much ground upwind as possible.

There are two methods of efficient tacking. The first is the 'fast tack' in which the board's momentum is maintained throughout the turn; and the 'quick tack' where the idea is to alter course as quickly as possible, regardless of the loss of speed.

Fast tacking requires a good deal of initial speed and a long smooth arc; whereas the quick tack requires a sharp turn. Neither method will be successful, however, unless it includes a carefully timed and smoothly executed rig change-

5. Move quickly around the front of the board, swapping your hands on the mast as you go.

6. Throw the rig forward with your new mast hand and place your other hand on the boom.

4. When the board is pointing directly upwind, place your front foot in front of the mast.

3. Continue to sheet in until the sail is over the centreline of the board.

over. Don't oversheet when you are luffing up and don't change sides until the board is genuinely facing into the wind. Try to leave the sail empty for the minimum amount of time. If you are on a low-volume board, keep your weight back near the mast as much as you can when you step around the rig, to prevent the board heading underwater like a submarine.

If you are tacking you will probably be sailing on an upwind course (beating). Choosing when to tack has as much influence on your overall speed upwind as the tacking manoeuvre itself. For example, if the wind is very gusty and coming from one direction and then another (shifting) it could be worth tacking each time you are 'headed', i.e. when the wind swings to blow from the front of the board and you are forced to bear off. If the opposite happens and you are 'lifted' and able to point higher then stay on the same tack. In steady winds, minimize the number of tacks as each will slow you down.

Never sail past the point at which your destination is directly behind you. In racing, you would be on the 'lay line' and able to sail a direct course to the mark. If your destination is not directly upwind, always make the direct tack (rather than the cross tack) the longer one.

When sailing close-hauled, keep the dagger down and the leeward rail slightly dipped and don't sacrifice too much speed in favour of pointing ability.

7. Sheet in and help the board to bear off by pushing with your front foot.

8. Move back as the board picks up speed on the new tack.

2. Sheet in and keep your weight back to help the board turn up into the wind.

1. Begin the tack by raking the rig back. Put one hand on the mast.

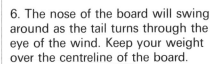

The Flare Gybe

The flare gybe was first developed as a freestyle trick. Because pressure is put on the tail and the windward rail, the nose of the board swings around rapidly, sometimes a couple of feet in the air. This can look quite spectacular and gets the freestylist onto a new tack quickly, ready to perform his next trick.

Today the flare gybe is the most advanced form of gybing for boards that don't footsteer, but its use has also been extended to the funboard and racing

7. You should now be sailing clew-first in the opposite direction.

6. The nose of the board will swing around as the tail turns through the eye of the wind. Keep your weight over the centreline of the board.

5. Continue to submerge the windward rail, balancing the board with your other foot.

4. The board should now start to turn downwind.

arenas. To the funboard sailor, flare gybing is a useful way of bringing the board onto a new tack when conditions are marginal and there is insufficient wind to keep the board 'carving' throughout the turn.

To the racing enthusiast, the flare gybe is a fast and efficient method of getting his board around a gybe mark, especially when a number of sailors are trying to round the buoy at the same time.

Basically, the flare gybe requires a sudden sinking of the tail combined with pressure on the windward (outside) rail. This slows the board down and, with the rig raked to windward, will swing the nose

around by almost 180 degrees and onto the new tack – in this case a starboard tack. The rig, which is now clew-first, is then allowed to flip around (see caption).

Before going into the gybe you should have your daggerboard down as the board will pivot round it. The radius of the turn is governed by the degree to which you sink the tail so the further aft you move your weight, the tighter the turn will be. In light winds this will be something of a balancing act but in strong winds it will help to slow the board down and give you increased control.

Remember to keep the windward rail

depressed throughout the turn. If you don't, the board will level out and sail in a straight line. As soon as the tail has turned through the wind, move your weight forward so that the tail is no longer submerged, producing extra drag and slowing the board down.

When you flip the rig, release your back (sail) hand first so that you can use it to grasp the mast and pull it forward as soon as you release your other hand.

As a method for learning the more complicated carve gybe, the flare gybe is ideal because the technique for flipping the rig is almost identical.

8. Move forward, place your back hand on the mast and allow the rig to flip around. Release your front hand as it goes.

9. Pull the rig forward across the front of your body and place your new back hand on the boom.

10. Transfer your new mast hand to the boom and sheet in.

3. Depress the windward rail with your foot and lean the rig to windward.

2. Move back to sink the tail and help the board to turn.

1. Begin the gybe by bearing off onto a broad reach.

Progressing to Higher Winds

In order to tackle strong winds you will have to master the use of footstraps. Along with footsteering, they open up the full spectrum of high-wind manoeuvres to the funboard sailor. To use the footstraps the board must be planing; that is, it must be moving fast enough to skim across the surface of the water rather than simply plough through it. In stronger winds, planing will be automatic but in marginal conditions (Force 3) you will have to initiate the plane yourself.

Begin by sailing on a reach (the fastest point of sailing) with the daggerboard retracted. Trim the board with the mast track forward and keep the board flat so that the maximum area is presented to the water (this produces maximum lift).

The sail should also be trimmed correctly – not under-sheeted so that it luffs, or over-sheeted so that it stalls as the leeward airflow detaches. Pumping the sail will help, especially as a gust comes along. This is done by pushing and pulling on the sail as if you were doing press-ups on the boom. You will learn to recognize the approach of a gust by watching for tell-tale patches of ripples on

the surface of the water. Don't attempt to move back and put your feet in the straps too soon: the tail will dig in, produce extra drag and prevent the board from planing properly. Once on the plane, try to anticipate a lull, bend your knees and put your weight forward on the mast foot. Or, if necessary, move forward out of the straps before the wind dies.

In stronger winds, getting your feet in the straps as soon as you can is a useful insurance against catapult falls. Put your back foot into the forward back strap first,

The correct stance for sailing in higher winds.

sheet in so that the board picks up speed and then slip your front foot into the appropriate strap.

Correct stance on a funboard is important. Don't stand square onto the centreline of the board but swing your body round to face the direction of travel, keeping the upper half of your body straight. This will make controlling the rig much more comfortable. Keeping your hands close together on the boom will make you more sensitive to changes in the wind so that you can trim the sail accordingly.

When sailing in higher winds it is important to lean out and rake the rig to windward when a gust hits. To prevent a catapult fall, pull in with your mast hand while spilling some of the wind with your back hand. If a particularly strong gust hits, it can push the centre of effort back in the sail, making the board head up into the wind. In extreme cases, the board can round up so much you will be pushed into the water on what was the windward side. Using a modern, stable rig will help to prevent this, of course, as will a retracted daggerboard, or even the use of a shorter board that will have a centre of lateral resistance much further back down its length. If you do find yourself un-avoidably luffing, try holding the boom further back and swing it forward slightly as you rake it to windward when counteracting the gust. This will keep the CE forward and help you to bear off. Be prepared for a burst of speed, however.

Footsteering

Once in the footstraps and planing comfortably in a strong wind, you can experiment with footsteering – the first step towards learning how to carve gybe.

Footsteering involves banking the board in the direction you want to turn. Your back foot should do most of the work. Digging in your heel while pulling up with the top of your back foot will steer the board to windward (pulling your front foot round to windward will help it turn). On the other hand, putting pressure on the leeward rail with your toes and the ball of your back foot while lifting with your front foot will turn the board away from the wind.

The pressure required will depend on a number of factors: the proximity of your back foot to the rear and edge of the board, your speed, and the design of the board itself. The nearer your foot is to the rear of the board, the easier it will be to sink the tail, but the faster the board is travelling, the greater the pressure you will have to exert in order to overcome the flow of water beneath the tail. Wide tails will require a greater amount of pressure but will turn tightly. Long narrow tails

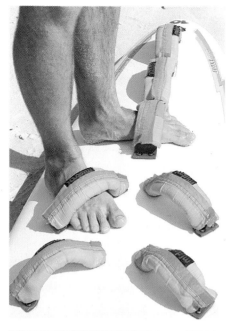

Left: Footstraps should be correctly adjusted so that each foot fits comfortably and securely. Ideally, your little toe should just protrude. Beware of straps that are too large: your foot could slip through during a wipe-out and your ankle be seriously damaged.

Below: An arm-wrenching catapult fall may look spectacular but if you fall onto the nose of the board or the rig, you could injure yourself or damage the sail. As soon as you realize a catapult is inevitable it is better to release the rig so that you fall to windward.

will be easy to sink but will turn through a wider arc.

To make a minor course adjustment, you can generally keep your back foot in the straps, but to execute a full-scale carving turn you will need to remove your back foot in order to exert maximum pressure on the rail.

Above: To footsteer a board, the daggerboard must be retracted and the board must be planing. The board is banked into the turn by putting pressure on the *inside* rail. The position of the rig has little influence on the turn.

SECTION THREE

HIGH PERFORMANCE WINDSURFING

When Hoyle Schweitzer first invented the term 'windsurfing,' he probably didn't realize just how accurately it would describe the high-performance end of the sport today. His original *Windsurfer* was modelled on a Malibu surfboard of the type popular in the 1950s, but in operation it was very similar to a conventional sailing craft. Today's more advanced boards have turned a full circle and now work in a fashion similar to real surfboards. They usually have no daggerboards; they are designed to perform efficiently under planing conditions and the sailor uses his feet, rather than the sail, to steer the board.

Except for some long, sleek race boards that are designed to go upwind easily, high-performance windsurfing really describes the use of short boards. Short boards can be any length from 3.20m (10ft 6in) to 2.4m (7ft 6in) or less and are very similar in shape to surfboards. Because of their small wetted surface, reduced length and light weight, short boards are fast, manoeuvrable and easy to handle in waves and high winds.

Before you discover the joys of sailing on a high-performance short board, you will have to learn to water start – uphauling a low-volume short board can be difficult and sometimes impossible. Once learned, it is a short step to high-speed carve gybing, jumping and wave riding – what some would call true windsurfing. All these manoeuvres can be performed on a long board with the daggerboard retracted, but just as an aerobatic plane will outperform a passenger jet, so a short board will complete a high-speed manoeuvre faster and more effectively than its longer cousin.

World Champion Robby Naish getting considerable 'airtime' off the huge waves of that windsurfing mecca, Hawaii.

ADVANCED EQUIPMENT

All high-performance boards are designed to perform at their best in moderate to strong winds (Force 4 and beyond). The sailing characteristics that concern a board designer or 'shaper' include acceleration (i.e. the propensity of a board to plane quickly), speed in a given wind strength, directional stability and turning, jumping and upwind sailing abilities.

There is no single blueprint for the ideal high-performance board and most shapers are forced to juggle with a number of different design criteria in order to make a board for a particular purpose or one that is suited to certain conditions. A short, narrow speed board, or 'gun', for example, may be the fastest board on a reach, but it would be unable to out-perform a wider and more manoeuvrable board on the waves. Neither board would beat a longer race board around a triangular course due to their inability to sail well upwind.

Plan shape

The plan shape of a board encompasses its length, width and 'rail curve'. Obviously, the longer the board, the more volume and stability it will have (and consequently less manoeuvrability) but length must always be considered in relation to width. A long narrow board will have good upwind ability due to its long waterline length, and a short narrow board will be very fast due to its reduced wetted area and minimal drag.

The position of the wide point, which influences the rail curve (i.e. the shape of the board when viewed from above) is another important design consideration. A board with a wide point slightly forward of its centre will have a long-drawn-out tail. This will make it fast and stable when travelling at speed but acceleration will be slow (due to the lack of lift in the rear of the board to help it onto the plane) and it will perform long

High-performance boards: note the different wide points and tail shapes.

drawn-out turns. As the wide point is pulled back, speed and directional stability are sacrificed for quick planing and sharper turns.

Rocker

Rocker is the amount of curvature in the board when viewed from the side. With the exception of 'nose scoop' (which prevents the nose from ploughing into the water ahead), rocker, or bottom curve, also influences the speed and turning ability of a board. Excessive rocker in the mid-section and rear of the board will make it turn easily; this is because the board will have a smaller area on which to pivot and the curve of the board when it is banked over will help to guide it through the turn. But, when travelling in a straight line, the extra curve in the planing surface

will cause extra drag. Conversely, a very flat board with negligible rocker will be very fast but hard to turn.

Volume and volume distribution

All high-performance boards will have relatively low volumes – either because they are long and narrow or because they are short. A high volume makes it difficult to sink the tail in turns, and at speed it will make the board bounce across the surface. However, the exact amount of volume in a board should be considered in the light of the conditions in which it is to be used and on the weight of the sailor. For example, a board with a relatively high volume for its length will be suitable for a heavy sailor with enough weight to sink the rails and tail during a turn.

Volume distribution is another factor crucial to the handling of a board. Too much volume in the rear section will make it difficult to sink the rails and tail so that they bite into the water and carve the board round a turn. The wider the board

Tail Shapes *Below right*

Pintail: provides smooth handling at speed but is slow to plane.

Rounded pintail: the pin shape gives a clean water release while the extra width provides added lift.

Squash tail: generates lots of lift, jumps well and turns sharply, but it is difficult to sink easily.

Diamond tail: similar to a squash tail but with slightly less lift and slightly more sink. The point provides better water release.

Swallow tail: the theory behind this is that it produces lots of lift but when banked into the turn only one tail need be sunk.

Asymmetric tail: the pintail side lends itself to fast drawn-out bottom turns while the squash tail side allows slower, sharper cutbacks.

Wings: these allow the designer to build in width near the tail and can provide pivot points during turns.

(from rail to rail), the thinner it needs to be to keep the volume down. On the other hand, there should be sufficient volume in the mid-section to prevent the rig from pushing the nose underwater.

Rails

Rail configuration has a significant effect on the turning characteristics of a board. 'Hard' or 'sharp' rails bite into the water efficiently – especially at speed – and are generally used in the tail section to increase turning efficiency. The mid-section of the board usually has softer, more rounded rails that won't dig in during the turn and 'trip up' the board.

Water tends to stick to curved rails as it flows around them, creating a force similar to surface tension that holds the board in the water. It is sometimes necessary therefore to give the rails a more efficient water-release edge for speed and quick planing – especially on shorter boards. This is achieved by giving each rail a 'tucked-under edge', i.e. a sharp edge underneath the smoothly curving rail. Thus, the edge releases water efficiently until the board is banked, and the water then sticks to the rail holding the board into the water during a turn.

Bottom contours

In order to facilitate water flow underneath the hull, most high-performance boards will have a number of grooves and channels built into them. These have various effects: concaves running the length of the board and flattening out near the tail will trap air and water and allow the board to plane more easily. Once planing, both single and double

concaves reduce the wetted surface, thereby reducing drag and increasing speed. Single concaves and air scoops in the front section absorb the slamming effect felt when the board is travelling through choppy water. 'Vee' used toward the back of the board makes rail to rail transitions easier and directs turbulent, aerated water away from the fin. It also makes the board 'looser' and slower to plane. Vee used in the front section (and in between double concaves) helps the board cut through chop and sail upwind. Channels used in the aft section of the board work in much the same way as concaves but also loosen up the turns.

Tails

Where short boards are concerned, the tail section is the most crucial aspect of board design. It not only influences the board's turning qualities, it also affects its speed, planing and jumping characteristics as well. A wide tail allows the board to turn sharply, accelerate quickly and jump easily, but it will also make it difficult to handle in higher winds as it will bounce over chop and spin out in turns.

A long narrow tail will be slow to plane (due to the small amount of lift it provides) but the board will then be much faster and stable at high speeds. Turns will be longer and more drawn out but less prone to cavitation and spin out.

Tail design is therefore something of a compromise between width, which generates lift; length, which provides clean water release and stability; and low volume, which makes it easier to sink during turns. As with almost all aspects of board design, different shapes are suitable

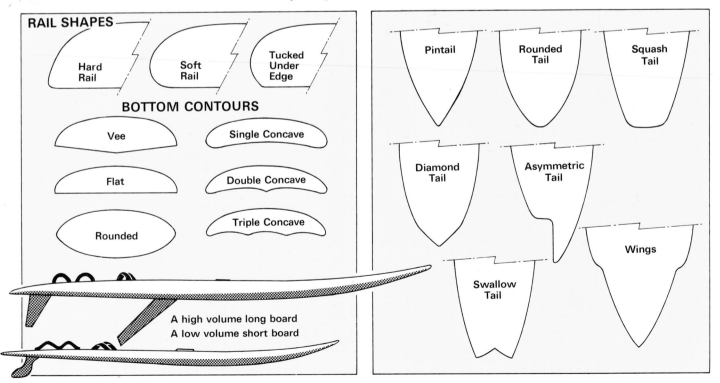

RAIL SHAPES — Hard Rail, Soft Rail, Tucked Under Edge

BOTTOM CONTOURS — Vee, Single Concave, Flat, Double Concave, Rounded, Triple Concave

A high volume long board
A low volume short board

Pintail, Rounded Tail, Squash Tail, Diamond Tail, Asymmetric Tail, Swallow Tail, Wings

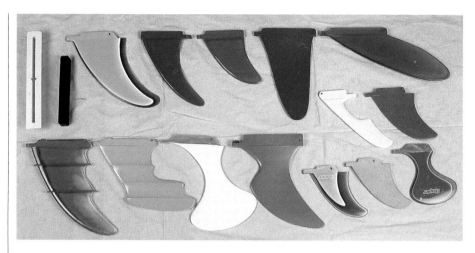

Left: Fins come in an enormous variety of shapes and sizes, although all will fit into the standard fin box (top left). Most designs are intended to minimize cavitation, either through the use of thin 'necks' or 'fences'.

Below: One essential piece of equipment on fragile glass fibre or epoxy boards is a mast pad. This prevents the mast from damaging the deck during a fall.

Above: Thruster fins can be added to short boards to aid stability, especially during turns.

for different conditions and different sailing styles. The diagram illustrates most of the common shapes in use today.

Wings

On shorter boards, wings are used to narrow the tail suddenly in order to reduce its volume, while still maintaining enough width (and hence lift) sufficiently near the tail itself. Some wide boards have two sets of wings. Wings on some boards are designed to act as little pivot points during turns.

Asymmetrical boards

Because different boards and tail shapes behave in different ways, some specialized boards are asymmetrical, i.e. one side has a different plan shape from the other. To the wave rider this means he can have the optimal tail shape for making fast drawn-out bottom turns, yet still have the ideal tail shape for the slower cutback at the top of the wave. Of course, this only works on one particular tack, so when the wind changes direction another board with the opposite tail configuration is required.

Materials

High-performance boards can be made in any of the four materials normally used in sailboard construction: Polyethylene, ASA, GRP and epoxy. All custom and short-run moulded boards (pop-outs) are made in GRP using either polyester or epoxy resins and either standard glass-fibre cloth or the stronger but more expensive Kevlar and carbon fibre. Some production boards from the major manufacturers are made in polyethylene or ASA but the majority today are made in epoxy.

The advantages of epoxy construction lie in the fact that it produces a stiff, lightweight board with a smooth finish. A light weight makes a board much more manoeuvrable while extra stiffness ensures that the power of the rig is transformed into speed. Polyethylene boards, for example, tend to flex as they

travel through the water and waste precious energy. Even some epoxy boards have added reinforcement, often in the form of carbon fibre, which increases stiffness without significantly increasing weight.

The disadvantage of both epoxy and standard GRP construction is fragility. GRP boards often suffer from 'dings' (small dents) and may shatter or crack if they hit a hard object. Epoxy boards are also expensive.

Materials research is a fast-moving part of the sailboard industry today and hybrid materials are constantly being experimented with in the search for ideal strength, weight, durability – and, of course, price.

Fins

The purpose of a fin is to provide lateral resistance and directional stability. The number, size, type and position of fins will each affect a board's performance.

A fin moved forward in its box will make the board looser in turns (it moves the pivot point forward), while a fin position closer to the tail will increase directional stability at speed.

Problems arise with fins in the area of spin out. Apart from the 'spin out' that is actually caused by a sailor's bad technique, there are two types of spin out. The first occurs at speed (or on landing from a jump) when the fins suffer from cavitation (i.e. when aerated water flows down the fin, causing it to lose its grip, and the board to slide sideways). In its other form, spin out occurs when the board is cranked over too hard during a turn and the fin pops out of the water, again causing the board to slip sideways. This is usually limited to wide-tailed boards where the distance from the rail to the fin is greater than on a narrow-tailed board. Many strange and unusual fins have been designed to reduce the likelihood of cavitation, usually by preventing aerated water from moving down the fin (see photo).

Small thruster or tracker fins set on either side of the main fin are designed to aid stability and control on short boards travelling at speed, on landing from jumps and during turns when at least one of them will be in the water (although there is a danger of fins hydroplaning). Thrusters have other other advantages: they can be 'toed in' to guide a board around the turn and they can be set up asymmetrically by altering the size and position of each fin so that the board behaves in a similar fashion to a true asymmetric board.

The best fins are hand made and constructed in GRP. Polycarbonate and other plastic fins are cheaper but not as stiff. Rigidity is a desirable characteristic in a fin, but a small amount of flex at the tip is useful to make it slightly more giving.

When installing a fin, make sure you use a nylon or soft-metal screw that will give under pressure (should you hit a submerged object or run aground) before any damage is done to the fin box itself.

Top: A high-aspect sail designed for wave-riding.
Above: Note the different profiles of a slalom sail (left) and a wave-sail (right).

High-Performance Sails

The sailboard rig has been the subject of much research and development over recent years and it is only now that particular categories of high-performance sails are beginning to emerge from the numerous advances in sailmaking technology. In the same way that board designers shape boards to suit different uses and conditions – short wide boards for wave riding, long sleek 'guns' for fast reaching and slalom racing, and long fast boards for course racing – so sailmakers are now designing sails to suit the same categories of sailing.

The leading edge

The all important factor in the operation of a sail is the airflow over its surface. The luff, or leading edge of the sail, influences how cleanly the sail cuts through the air, and therefore how smoothly the 'attached' airflow flows towards the leech and foot, or trailing edges. Conventional sails have loose luff pockets that produce 'holes' behind the mast and disrupt the airflow. This can lead to a 20 per cent loss of efficiency when compared to a more aerodynamic leading edge.

The first solution to this problem was the 'wing' mast, named after its similarity to a long thin wing. Rather than have a luff sleeve, the sail was attached to a track on the trailing edge of the mast. This was a radical departure from the conventional tubular mast and, although it provided a highly efficient leading edge for the sail, it wasn't practical for normal sailing due to its excessive weight, lack of strength and high cost. In theory the clean entry that the wing mast provided was ideal and so designers set about producing more practical versions of the wing-mast idea.

Rotational sails. These are also called rotating asymmetrical foils, or RAF sails. By placing full-length battens in the sail so that they sit on the side of the mast, rather than behind it, designers are able to simulate the leeward surface of a wing mast (i.e. an asymmetrical 'wing' or foil shape). The original wing mast was articulated and could be adjusted to produce the correct angle of attack depending on which tack the sail was on. Rotational sails rotate around the mast as the wind moves round to blow from the other side of the sail during a tack or a gybe. In practice, the battens 'snap' around as the sail flips onto the new tack.

Camber induced sails. These have wide luff sleeves supported by 'camber inducers'. A camber inducer is a 'Y'-shaped plastic device that rotates around the mast at its forked end and supports a batten at the other. In this way the designer is able to build smooth leeward and windward leading edges into the luff of the sail and keep the point of maximum camber forward. The camber-induced sail is more efficient than a rotational one but it is usually heavier and less manoeuvrable.

Split battens. Battens with split ends can be inserted into a sail with a wide luff sleeve, so that the split section supports the sleeve on both sides and forms a foil shape.

Foam sleeves. Another way of simulating the original wing mast is to insert a foil-shaped length of foam into the luff sleeve. This surrounds the mast itself and produces a 'soft' wing mast.

Battens

Full-length battens are used in nearly all high-performance rigs to support the sail and help it to maintain a stable shape. The best type of batten is tapered – thick at one end and thin at the other, so that it has different flex characteristics along its length. The thin end bends easily and helps to keep the camber forward in the sail, while the thick end remains flat and holds out the leech area.

Profile and shape

Most modern sails are high aspect, i.e. they have relatively short booms and high clews compared to the all-round regatta sails of the past. A high clew won't drag in the water while gybing or wave riding (wave sails have the highest clews of all) and the thinner profile of a high clew sail means that the point of maximum camber is closer to the mast than normal. This makes the sail more manageable.

Foot battens have allowed sailmakers to add extra area to high-clew sails without making the mast so long that it becomes too flexible at its tip. This extra area under the boom also helps the sailors to close the inefficient gap between the foot of the sail and the deck of his board as he rakes the rig back in a high wind.

By stitching the panels together in a certain way, the sailmaker can build a pre-determined amount of camber into a sail (although this can be adjusted to a certain extent by the sailor during the rigging process). A flat sail with a centre of effort forward will be easier to sail in heavy winds and gusty conditions, whereas a full sail will have more camber further back, producing extra power but less manoeuvrability and overall control.

Materials

In common with most man-made materials, sail cloth is undergoing continual change and development. Stretch-resistant polyester film laminates such as Mylar are now common to all high-performance sails. Because these materials don't stretch significantly during gusts or after heavy use, the centre of effort in the sail is prevented from moving back and making control difficult.

Rather than use a single material in a particular sail, sailmakers often use various types, weights and densities in different parts of the sail. For example, double-ply Mylar is frequently used in the highly stressed areas, such as along the leech and foot and around the tack, clew

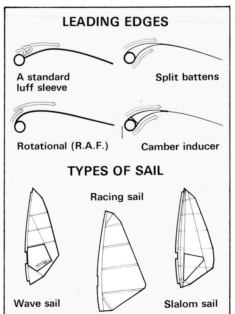

LEADING EDGES

A standard luff sleeve

Split battens

Rotational (R.A.F.)

Camber inducer

TYPES OF SAIL

Racing sail

Wave sail

Slalom sail

A camber induced sail. Note how the draught is well forward.

The original wing mast.

Racing sails. Note the long booms combined with full length battens.

and head. Lightweight Mylar is used in the body of the sail to keep its weight down. Even Dacron is sometimes used in the luff area, where a degree of flexibility is an advantage.

Types of sail

Modern high-performance sails are designed for a particular use and although the following rough categories overlap to a certain extent, most sails fall into one of them.

Wave sails. As the name suggests, a wave sail is designed for use in waves where ease of handling is more important than sheer power. This type of sail is characterized by a long mast, a short boom, a high clew and a flat cut. There are two schools of thought as ·to whether a 'hard' fully battened, super flat sail is better in the waves than a 'soft' short-battened sail with more power, but less controllability. The choice depends on the sailor and his sailing style.

Some sails are sold with a dual-batten system which allows the use of either short or full-length battens in the same pocket so that the sailor can choose between a hard, rotational sail and a soft sail depending on the conditions and his preferences.

Slalom sails. These feature longer booms and a fuller cut and are half way between wave sails and full-blown racing sails. The ideal sail for slalom racing, or just high-wind recreational sailing, has extra power for quick acceleration and fast reaching, combined with light weight and manoeuvrability for easy gybing and water starting.

Some slalom sails are rotational – it is felt that this type of design combines

maximum power and stability with light weight – but some have camber inducers or split battens for an added turn of speed.

Racing sails. Speed, pointing ability and performance over a wide range of wind strengths are the desirable characteristics in a racing sail. And for those who relish pure fast reaching, this sort of sail is ideal. Racing sails have lower aspect ratios than most high-performance sails and are cut full to take maximum advantage of the wind speed. The dominant leading edge in this category is camber-induced. The problem with a camber-induced sail is that it is heavy – making control difficult, especially in light winds – and that the wide luff sleeve fills with water, so that it makes uphauling and water starting difficult.

Tuning a high-performance sail

A high-performance sailboard rig should always be regarded as a single unit, the mast sail and boom working in harmony with one another. The mast should always be stiff enough for the sail and should always have the correct flex characteristics (every sail is cut for a particular mast), otherwise it may be impossible to set the sail without wrinkles and creases. Booms should also be stiff and the correct width for the sail: wide for full cut, rotational or camber-induced sails, but thinner for flat-cut wave sails. Be sure to adjust the length of the boom so that it fits the width of the sail.

There can be up to four tuning controls on a high-performance sail: the inhaul, the downhaul (which should each incorporate a pulley system), the batten

tensioning straps and the tack strap (this influences the distance that the tack of the sail can 'float' away from the mast).

The rigging and tuning sequence is as follows:
1 Tension the downhaul
2 Tension the outhaul
3 Secure the tack strap
4 Fine tune the sail with the outhaul and downhaul
5 Tension the battens to suit the trim of the sail.

Tuning a high-performance rig is not just a matter of applying maximum tension to the downhaul and then the outhaul. Each should be alternately tensioned in small stages until the desired shape is reached. When de-rigging (which is virtually the reverse of the rigging sequence), it is important to release the outhaul before the downhaul to avoid unduly stressing the tack and luff areas and possibly tearing a seam or two.

Sails made with polyester laminates such as Mylar need a great deal of care and attention if they are to remain in tip-top condition. Don't leave a Mylar sail fully rigged on an abrasive surface such as a car park as the areas in contact with the ground (the batten pockets in particular) will quickly wear away. Always wash a Mylar sail in fresh water before rolling it up and storing it in a sail bag. Ultra violet light and salt water combine to damage the synthetic materials in the sail and folding it will eventually result in cracks along the creases. If the stitching frays or the sail develops small tears, repair them temporarily with Mylar repair tape but take the sail for a full repair by a skilled sailmaker before the tears get worse.

ADVANCED TECHNIQUE

Water Starting

Water starting is the key that opens the door to short-board sailing and true high-performance windsurfing. Due to their low volumes, boards under 3.2m (10ft) or so become increasingly difficult to uphaul as they get shorter. It is virtually impossible to uphaul the rig on sinkers, and even on some marginals if you are above average weight.

It is often the case that the water start is also a much more efficient and energy-saving method of getting a long board underway.

Learning to water start is like learning to ride a bicycle: once you've mastered it you'll wonder why it took you so long to get it right. When attempting their first water start, most people assume that it is merely a matter of allowing the sail to pull them out of the water. On the contrary, the procedure starts much earlier and most people fail even before they have got the rig out of the water. There are various preparations to make before you can be sure that that final yank out of the water will be successful.

Obviously you'll need wind, a minimum of a Force 4 if you are of average weight. Generally speaking, the more wind the better, although this can complicate matters when you are trying to get the rig out of the water. Always learn on a long board. Ironically, water starting a short board is not as difficult. It is easier to manoeuvre into the right position, but when you tire and your arms and legs start to ache, at least you will be able to uphaul the rig on a long board and return to shore. To make life easier, try learning in shallow water so that you can stand up and rest if necessary. A modern, high-aspect sail will help because it will provide more leverage, and if it has a short boom, the likelihood of the clew catching in the water and acting as a pivot for the rest of the sail as it is wrenched from your grasp and flipped over by the wind will be reduced.

To the non-water-starting boardsailor, falling to windward with the rig causes unwelcome problems: either the rig has to be dragged across the board or the board itself has to be turned around before it can be uphauled in the normal manner. If you can water start, a rig to windward is the ideal situation from which to get going within a few seconds.

Obviously, the rig is not always going to fall conveniently to windward. Depending on which way it does fall, and on which direction your board is facing, there are various methods of getting it into the correct position. These are: i) swimming the board around; ii) swimming the rig around; iii) flipping the rig or (iv) a combination of any of these three. The box on page 61 illustrates when each is used.

The water start

Below left: Position the mast at right angles to the wind with the board upwind. Grip the mast above the boom and pull it up and over your head as you swim to windward so that the wind gets underneath the sail and the clew flies free.

Below: Grasp the boom with your other hand. In a very strong wind keep the luff low so that the clew doesn't catch in the water and sink.

Top left: Continue to kick your feet as if swimming towards the nose of the board, pushing down on the mast foot at the same time. This should bring the board onto a broad reach as it pivots around the skeg. (If you have a daggerboard, make sure it is retracted.)

Top right: Once the board is on the correct heading, lie back in the water and bring your back foot up onto the board – but not too close to the tail or it will sink as you stand up.

Middle left: Stretch your arms up as high as you can so that you present as much sail area to the wind as possible. At the same time tread water with your free foot to assist the sail.

Middle right: Rather than haul yourself up on the boom, try to use all your energy to 'step' up onto the board, and the rig should do the rest.

Bottom left: Keep your weight forward and on the mast foot to trim the board and allow it to pick up speed. Get your trailing leg onto the board as soon as you can in order to reduce drag.

Bottom right: Once you are up and going, remember to sheet out, or the same wind that picked you out of the water will throw you in on the other side.

These methods should put you in the ideal position to water start: that is with the mast at 90 degrees to the wind (and the clew downwind) and the board facing into the wind. From there it is just a matter of practice and perseverance to lift the rig, head the board on a reach, hook your foot onto the board and let the sail lift you out of the water.

However, some problems can arise. If you can't get the rig out of the water initially, try swimming backwards and using both hands to pull the mast out of the water and into the wind. Sometimes, the clew doesn't fly free or catches in the water again. The wind then gets under the luff, forcing it into the air and the clew underwater. If using all your strength and weight to hold it down until the clew comes free again doesn't work, just let the boom go, pull up on the boom (which will now be almost vertical) so that the clew comes to the surface but this time to windward of the mast. Let the wind flip it downwind so that you can start again.

Another problem arises when you put your foot onto the board and the nose of the board starts to head upwind. Cure this by swimming the rig towards the nose and by putting pressure on the boom with your forward hand, this should swing the nose back downwind again.

Catapulting over the other side of the board as soon as you are out of the water usually spoils your first water start. This could be the result of facing the board too far downwind, but it is more likely to be

due to the fact that you didn't trim the sail correctly. Remember to sheet out slightly once you are up and moving.

The water start is probably the most difficult windsurfing technique to master but it is also the most essential if you want to get the most out of the sport. Without it, short-board sailing is impossible and long-board sailing in extreme conditions is dangerous; but with it, you can be up and sailing within seconds – crucial seconds that could win a race or get you out of the way of a huge breaking wave.

The light-wind water start

There are going to be occasions during your windsurfing career when the wind drops and you find yourself on a sinker or a board that cannot easily be uphauled. If you don't want to paddle all the way back to shore after a fall, the light-wind water start is a useful skill to acquire.

In essence, it is no different from the standard water start except that a much larger sail area is presented to the wind in the early stages of the manoeuvre. The photographs show the light-wind water start in its most extreme form, but there is a technique that doesn't go as far: in this the sailor holds the mast with his front hand and the boom with his back hand (rather than the foot of the sail).

In either version it is important to kick hard with your trailing leg and keep as close to the board as possible. Once on the board, keep away from the tail and pump hard to get the board moving.

The light-wind water start.

Top left: Raise the rig as you would for a normal water start and head the board downwind on a reach. Place your front hand on the mast.

Above left: While carefully balancing the rig against the wind, grab the foot of the sail with your back hand.

Above: Use your back hand to sheet in and out while you place your back foot on the board.

Opposite top: Bring your front foot on so that you are almost in a sitting position with the rig upright. Spread your weight so that the board remains properly trimmed.

Opposite top right: As soon as the board starts to make headway, stand up.

Opposite far right: Transfer your hands to the boom (back hand first) and sail off as normal.

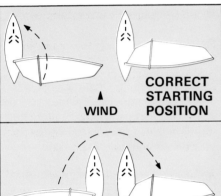

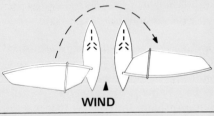

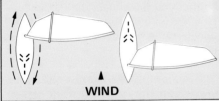

CORRECT STARTING POSITION

WIND

WIND

WIND

WIND

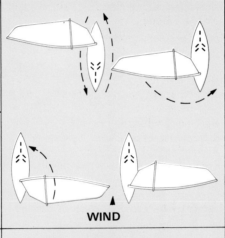

One of the most difficult aspects of water starting after a fall is returning the board and rig to the correct starting position (board pointing into the wind, mast in the water at right angles to the board, clew downwind). Any or all of the following may be wrong: the clew may be facing into the wind; the rig may be on the wrong side of the board; or the board itself may be pointing in the wrong direction.

Clew facing upwind: lift the clew so that it catches the wind and flips over.
Rig on the wrong side of the board: lift up the rig by the mast and swim it round.
Board out of position: a short board can be spun around by sinking the nose as it passes under the rig. If you are on a longer board, it is a better idea to manoeuvre the rig first so that you can either start in the opposite direction or drag the rig over the tail of the board if you want to start on a particular tack.
Board and rig out of position, clew upwind: Spin the board around first, swing the rig around and then flip the clew.

Left: How to return the board to the correct starting position.

High-Speed Gybing

Flying along on a fast reach, leaning your body into a powerful banking turn, and driving your board through a properly carved gybe is one of the most exhilarating feelings you will ever experience on a board. Most high-performance boardsailors probably spend more time gybing than they do on all other windsurfing manoeuvres put together. Of course, the purpose of a gybe is to change direction, whether it be in order to round a buoy during a slalom race, or to ride the waves back in, having jumped them on the way out. However, high-speed gybing can be so stimulating that it is more often than not carried out purely for its own sake.

Gybing a funboard of any length differs from the standard flare gybe in two important ways. First of all, the board should be kept planing throughout the turn, and not stalled as in a flare gybe. And secondly, assuming your board will footsteer, the deck is presented to the inside of the turn as the board is carved around, rather than to the outside of the turn as in a flare gybe.

The classic carve gybe is the standard method of gybing in strong winds, and whereas the duck gybe, and its variant the one-handed duck gybe, look much more fluid (if performed properly), they are more difficult to master. The scissors, or slam gybe, is the odd one out as it is a very specialized manoeuvre and only really used to get the sailor out of a tricky situation.

With the exception of the scissors gybe (which is more akin to a high-performance flare gybe), all high-wind gybes should be judged, not by the speed with which you begin them, but by the speed at which you complete them. Going into the gybe half-heartedly and not really committing yourself to the turn will inevitably result in failure.

Basically, all high-wind gybes involve banking the board through the turn and flipping the rig in some way. It is the difference in the methods used to get the rig onto the opposite tack that distinguishes the carve gybe from the duck gybe. In a carve gybe the rig is swung around the nose of the board in a fashion similar to that used for the flare gybe. In the duck gybe, the sailor literally ducks

The carve gybe

Left: Approach the gybe on a beam reach, remembering to unhook your harness. Remove your back foot from the strap and place it near the leeward rail.

Below left: Apply pressure with your back foot so that the rear section of the leeward rail bites and begins to initiate the carve. Pull up with your forward foot (which should still be in its strap) in order to help the board bank.

Opposite, top row: Lean into the turn and keep your knees bent. This aids stability and control as it keeps your centre of gravity low; it allows you to absorb the jarring effects of any chop and it makes it easy to adjust the degrees of bank.

Middle left: You should now have passed the dead downwind position with the rig going clew-first. Sheet out to increase the power in the sail and maintain pressure on the leeward rail to keep the board carving. Move your front hand towards the mast end of the boom and then release your back hand.

Middle right: Grip the mast with your back hand and allow the rig to swing around across the nose of the board. Release your other hand as it goes.

Bottom left: As the boom comes around grab it with your free hand and push the mast forward with your other hand. Continue to dig the leeward rail into the water until the board is back on a reach.

Bottom right: Sheet in and reverse the position of your feet: your back foot is moved forward and your front foot is moved back.

under the sail as the tail of the board passes through the eye of the wind.

Before attempting any high-wind gybe, take note of the following: if you have a daggerboard, ensure it is fully retracted – otherwise it will prevent the board from carving properly. Choppy water and approaching swells will quickly slow the board down and make it stall, so try to choose a relatively flat and smooth patch of water. Also, a planing funboard is controlled by your feet, rather than by the sail, so you must really *use* your feet during a gybe. On the other hand, don't oversteer or try to carve too sharply. A correctly carved gybe should describe a fairly long smooth arc without the board coming off the plane. The actual diameter of the arc will vary according to the type of board you are sailing.

The carve gybe

The essence of a good carve gybe is to keep the board carving throughout the turn and to time the rig change correctly. In very high winds you can start to release the rig when you are dead downwind, as your speed and momentum should carry you through the remaining part of the turn before you sheet in on the other tack.

In more marginal conditions, however (where you are in danger of coming off the plane), it is important not to release the rig until you are sailing clew-first and then flip the rig as quickly and efficiently as you can, minimizing the time when there is no power in the sail.

The duck gybe

During the duck gybe, the rig change takes place much earlier and good timing is even more essential. Ducking under the rig while you are heading directly downwind means that the apparent wind in the sail will be negligible, as you will be sailing at speed in the same direction as the wind itself. Nevertheless, try to prevent the mast from falling too far forward as this will make it harder to recover as you continue to carve around. When learning, you can use the foot of the sail as an intermediate stage if you can't make it a clean, boom-to-boom transition right away. Don't lose faith at this stage and reduce the bank: you will just end up sailing straight downwind to an eventual stop. Once you have flipped the rig successfully it is merely a matter of continuing the turn until you are heading on your new course.

The duck gybe

Top left: While sailing on a reach, bank the board into the turn by depressing the leeward (inside) rail with your back foot.

Top right: Move your front hand to a position behind your back hand on the boom.

Above left: Pull the rig over your head as the clew passes through the eye of the wind.

Above: Grasp the opposite boom with your free hand as quickly as you can.

The slam gybe

This is almost the same as a flare gybe except that it is generally performed on a shorter board and in a higher wind. It is used when you can't afford to sail around the relatively long arc required by the carve and duck gybes.

While heading on a reach, move towards the back of the board, sink the tail and rake the rig over your head in order to slow the board down considerably. Then pivot the board onto its new heading with your feet. You can either sail off clew first before flipping the rig or you can flip it as soon as the board is on its new heading.

Above left: And bring your other hand around onto the boom.

Top and above: It is important to continue the carve around by keeping pressure on the inside rail with your back foot, sheeting in as you do so until you are on a broad or beam reach again.

The one-handed duck gybe

As you pull the clew across the eye of the wind with your leading hand, you can drag your free hand in the water for a moment or two. This is really pure showmanship, although it does encourage you to lean into the turn!

The Body Drag

Tacking, gybing and water starting are all techniques with a specific purpose: to get you going or to change your direction. Some funboard manoeuvres have no real aim or objective, however, and are merely performed for the sailor's own amusement. One such trick is the body drag, seemingly pointless but great fun to try, especially if you manage to pull it off.

The essential requirement for a successful body drag is speed, and lots of it. The faster you are going when you step off the board the better. Not only will your body skim along the surface of the water more easily, your board will take longer to slow down, giving you extra time to step (or

The body drag

Top: With your dagger retracted, sail along on a beam reach as fast as you can. Remove your feet from the straps and step off the board front foot first.

Middle: Step off with your other foot and swing your body sideways so that you are dragged along on your thighs with your heels in the air. In this position you will present the least resistance and a good planing surface on the water.

Bottom: You will only be able to maintain this position for a split second as the board will slow down rapidly. Try and twist your body to get your front (windward) foot back onto the board.

even bounce!) back onto the board. Depending on your weight, 15 knots is about the minimum speed required.

Smooth water is useful of course, and a medium- or a longer-length board will make this trick easier than if performed on a short board – its lack of buoyancy could result in a nose dive with the extra weight on the rig. A longer board's bigger deck also presents a more stable landing platform.

Top: Try to keep as much weight on the mast foot as possible and sheet in to power the sail so that it pulls you onto the board.

Middle: With your front foot back on the board, you can put your weight on it while bringing up the other. Avoid stepping on the tail of the board as this will sink it and prevent you getting aboard again before it stalls.

Bottom: Once back on the board, the danger isn't over. All that power in the sail will catapult you over the nose unless you sheet out immediately to spill some of the wind. When you have recovered your balance you will have completed the body drag and possibly impressed a few friends back on the beach.

Sailing in Waves

Few sports can match the pure excitement and spectacle of windsurfing in waves and strong winds. The ability to punch out through the surf, jumping the waves on the way, before performing a smoothly carved gybe and riding the waves back in is the ultimate goal of most ambitious boardsailors.

Before reaching such a high level of performance, however, there is a lot to learn and beware of. Don't sail in large waves and high winds until you can water start; uphauling any length of board can be extremely difficult when heavy chop or breaking waves are doing their best to knock you off every few seconds. Learn to sail a short board on flat water before venturing out into surf conditions. Use good quality equipment and check it thoroughly before sailing. Avoid offshore winds and adverse currents; paddling through breaking waves after an equipment failure when the conditions are against you could prove impossible.

Reading waves

No two waves are identical but most fall into certain recognizable categories. Wind-induced chop is the most common and can even be found on larger stretches of inland water. It is impossible to ride chop but it can certainly be jumped. Properly formed waves are the result of weather conditions far out to sea. Storms generate ocean swells that travel towards land in 'sets' and, depending on the contours of the sea bottom, peak up and form waves that break (i.e. topple forward in a mass of white water) on or near the shore. Reefs, sand bars and points of land can all cause a wave to break.

The topography of the ocean bottom for some distance offshore governs the form a wave will take when it nears land. Steeply inclining sea bottoms produce fast moving, steep 'hollow'-faced waves such as those found in Hawaii and other tropical islands. Shallow continental shelves on the other hand tend to produce slower moving, less well-defined waves that are often described as 'mushy'.

Each part of a wave has a name. The 'lip' is the very tip of a wave that is just about to fall down the 'face'. The 'bottom' of a wave, as the name suggests, describes the base of a wave where it meets the trough. The part of a wave that has just broken is called the 'critical section'. Some waves break to the left, some to the right and some in two directions at once. Some waves 'close out' as two critical sections meet. The ability to 'read' a wave and anticipate what it is about to do is a necessary wave-sailing skill but it can only really be acquired through experience.

Wave jumping

Wave jumping is easier than it looks although you may not think so after your first few attempts! The precise technique varies according to conditions and your preferred style but there are two essential ingredients: speed and a suitable launching ramp. The face of a wave close to the critical section (but not too close!) will provide the perfect launching ramp. If the wave isn't breaking, then choose the steepest part of the face you can find.

Your first jump

1. Approach the wave at full speed and lean back as the board begins to take off.

2. Raising the windward rail will give the board extra lift as the wind gets underneath it.

3. Lift your heels and extend your front leg so that the tail of the board is pushed into the wind. This prevents luffing in mid-air and on landing. Trim the sail as for normal sailing.

4. Prepare for landing by extending your legs and sheeting out a bit to put the tail of the board in the water first.

5. As the board touches down, absorb the shock with your legs and, once the board is in the water, sheet in to continue sailing.

Right: In Hawaii, top wave-sailing professionals such as Pete Cabrinha can reach amazing heights. Pete takes off from the steepest part of the wave, pulls the rig over his head as the nose of the board points skyward, and then sheets out to prevent a nose-first landing.

Your speed will depend on the wind's strength – a Force 5 or more is necessary – and its precise direction.

A cross-shore wind is ideal as it means you can approach the wave head on while sailing on the fastest point of sailing, a beam reach. Directly onshore or offshore winds are useless for jumping. You can jump in cross-offshore and cross-onshore winds but they make life difficult. If the wind is cross-onshore you might have enough speed on a close reach but, if not, sail on a beam reach towards the wave, but head up at the last moment so that you still hit the wave head on.

In a cross-offshore, hitting the wave head on would put you on a broad reach (which encourages nose-diving after take-off) so you might have to sail on a beam reach for extra speed and hit the wave at an angle, so that you have enough power to launch the board into the air.

Far left: A high vertical jump.

Left: A flat distance jump.

Below far left: An upside down 'table top.

Below left: A 'donkey kick' from world champion Robby Naish.

There are three basic stages in a jump: the approach and take-off, your time in the air, and the landing. Assuming you are sailing in ideal conditions (a cross-shore wind and clean, steep waves) the basic technique is as follows: approach the wave at speed with your feet firmly in the straps but your harness unhooked. As your board travels up the face of the wave and the nose lifts off, shift your weight back and, if necessary, sheet out a little so that the board doesn't nose dive. As soon as you are in the air, kick your back foot (and hence the tail of the board) into the wind and pull the nose off the wind by extending your front leg. Lifting up your heels, especially the back one, helps the board to bear off a little in the air and puts you in a crouched but more controlled position. Trim the sail as necessary to prepare for the landing.

Until you have some experience of jumping, it is best to go for a tail-first landing. Landing slightly nose first will allow the board to plane easily after the

Below: A classic wave-riding sequence close to the critical section of a very large wave. The sailor bottom turns and then cuts back near the lip as it breaks just behind the tail of his board.

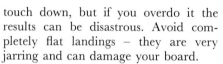

Chop jumping

Above: From a fast reach, head up towards the wind and lift the windward rail as the board takes off.

Above right: Hang from the boom and bend your knees to lift the tail out of the water. The wind will help to push the nose back onto a reach.

Right: Bring your weight forward to prevent a spin-out on landing. Note how the sail is trimmed for a reach – the fastest point of sailing – throughout the sequence.

touch down, but if you overdo it the results can be disastrous. Avoid completely flat landings – they are very jarring and can damage your board.

For a tail-first landing, sheet out and extend your legs to let the tail hit the water before the nose of the board, and absorb the impact by bending your knees. Try giving the rig a good hard pump as you land so that it acts as a parachute brake on your body. Spin out is a common problem on landing from a jump but it is easily solved by remembering to push the tail to windward while you are still airborne. Once you are safely in the water you can sheet in and continue to sail.

Once you have mastered the basic jump you can progress to more adventurous manoeuvres such as upside-down jumps and donkey kicks (in which your legs are kicked forcefully to windward while your upper body twists to maintain sail trim). The higher you go on a jump the more inverted you must become in order to avoid an extreme nose, down attitude on your descent. Hanging from the boom and using the sail as a parachute to break your fall will help.

Some experienced wave sailors are now able to get so high on a jump they are able to go all the way round and perform 360-degree barrel rolls or 'loops'.

If you get into trouble at any time during a jump, then don't hesitate to bail out. This is done by letting go of the boom with both hands and kicking your feet out of the straps so that the board drifts away from you in the air. A useful motto is: 'If in doubt, bail out.'

Chop jumping

Jumping in Force 5 cross-shore winds and cleanly breaking waves is relatively easy, but such ideal wind and water conditions rarely coincide (especially if you sail on inland water!) and you may have to be content with jumping wind-driven chop.

The trick is to head up slightly from a fast reach just as you spot a suitably steep piece of chop. As the nose of the board lifts, tilt the windward rail so that the wind gets underneath it and, with its help, lift your heels in a sort of springing action. In this way you can reach amazing heights from even the smallest chop. However, the smaller the chop the higher the wind really needs to be. A Force 5 is the minimum you will need.

Wave riding

Once you have jumped your way out to sea, you may want to ride the waves back in again. As with jumping, the ideal conditions for wave riding are cross-shore winds and clean, steep waves.

A bottom turn (note how well the leeward rail is sunk) . . . followed by a slashing top turn.

Riding waves on a sailboard is very similar to surfing on a conventional surfboard except that on a sailboard you have two sources of power – the wave as well as the wind. Your movment down the face of the wave can have a considerable effect on the apparent wind. So it is useful to have a fairly flat sail and be prepared to trim it correctly.

Basic wave riding is simple. Sheet out until your chosen wave approaches from behind, then sheet in so that you speed up and stay with the wave. This is called dropping in – the wave builds up behind you and lifts the tail of your board so that you are accelerated down the face.

Your objective is to stay on the wave and this may involve sheeting in or out depending on the size and speed of the wave and on the wind strength. You will probably be sailing in a cross-shore wind and therefore on a broad or beam reach. By heading up, you will slow down and move up the face of the wave, tracking across it towards the lip before bearing off again to accelerate down the face.

Once you have learnt to control the board on the face of the wave you can attempt some of the more advanced wave-riding manoeuvres:

The bottom turn

A fast turn made at the base of the wave in order to project the board along the wave or back up the face towards the lip. This sort of turn involves bearing the board away from the wind and sinking the leeward rail as hard as you can in order to avoid spinning out.

The top turn

As the name implies this is made at or near the top of the wave. After a bottom turn you will be rising up the face of the wave with the leeward rail depressed and your weight forward. By shifting your weight back, sheeting in and sinking both the tail and the windward rail, you can carve the board around to head back down the face of the wave again.

Off-the lip

This advanced manoeuvre is the same as a top turn except that it is made in the critical section of the wave. With precise timing the lip can be used to knock the underside of the board back down the wave. It is even possible to become airborne during this manoeuvre, in which case it is known as an aerial off-the-lip. The bigger the wave, the harder and more dangerous an off-the-lip becomes.

Gybing on a wave

Both carve gybes and duck gybes can be performed on the face of a wave. The trick is to judge the timing of your approach correctly so that you flip the rig while you are banking round on the face of the wave, parallel to the lip. The board's momentum will then be maintained as it drops down the wave.

These are just some of the more common wave-riding manoeuvres, enough to allow you to 'rollercoaster' up and down the face of a wave until it breaks and dies. You can then gybe, jump the waves on the way out and start again.

Above: An aerial off-the-lip.

Left: Dropping in on a wave.

Right: Surfing a wave. Note how the apparent wind swings round to make the sail 'back'.

Tacking a Short Board

Most short-board sailors avoid tacking – the gybe is a much more convenient and exciting manoeuvre. The low volume of the short boards, especially sinkers, makes them difficult to handle during a tack. As well as lacking lateral stability they tend to sink low in the water, and standing anywhere near the mast usually results in a nose dive. The shorter the board, the harder it is to tack.

Nevertheless, the ability to tack a very short board is a useful skill to have, especially when you have to sail upwind. Short-board sailing usually involves a good deal of reaching and gybing – exercises that can put you well downwind of your launching point.

The procedure for tacking a short board is similar to tacking a longer board but the following refinements will make your task easier. Complete the whole manoeuvre with as much speed as you can – the less time spent heading into the wind the better. Push with your feet to help the board come round quickly.

The secret is not to let the nose sink. By keeping your weight on your back foot you will keep the board in trim. Minimize the time your feet are near the mast; if you can, step over the mast as you lean the rig back or even jump around. If you can adjust your mast track, have it in the rear position.

Once onto the new tack, push down with your back foot (which should be well back down the board) in order to keep the nose from sinking. Get underway again as quickly as you can.

Tacking a short board

Below left: Head up into wind with as much speed as you can muster.

Below right: As the board slows down, lean the rig back and, keeping as much weight on your back foot as possible, step around the mast.

Bottom left: This is the crucial moment: swap hands on the mast and swing your body around, trying to put as little weight on the forward section as possible.

Bottom right: Get your back foot behind the front straps to keep the nose up and bear off quickly.

Speed sailing

Speed sailing is a branch of high-performance windsurfing that is becoming increasingly popular as the world sailboard speed record is pushed higher and higher. At the time of writing, it stands at over 32 knots and has been increased by 8 knots since 1980. Competitive speed-sailing events are held at specialized venues around the world that combine flat water with strong winds, but any calm and windy conditions will do to test your own speed-sailing skills.

The ability to sail fast is a combination of using the right equipment and finely tuning your sailing technique. Modern rigs are very aerodynamically efficient but the sheer size of the sail must be tempered to your ability to control it in high winds. It is no good having lots of power if you have to continually sheet out to spill some wind. Use a stiff mast, a rotational or camber-induced sail and a wide boom to give you good leaverage.

The smaller and thinner the board, the less weight and drag it will have on the water and the faster it will go. Specialist speed boards can be extremely narrow but any 'gun' or thin-tailed short board (around 3m – 9ft – or less) will be sufficient. Set your skeg in its rear position and keep the tack of the sail as close to the board as possible. Although they can't match the speeds of the fastest speed boards, multi-rigged boards such as tandems or tridems are very fast in average conditions. Sailing these is no different from sailing a normal board, although a tandem requires a good deal of co-ordination between the sailors.

The fastest point of sailing is a broad reach about 135 degrees off the wind (as you go faster the apparent wind swings around to blow more from the nose of the board). To squeeze those extra few knots

from your board you will have to keep it as level as possible, both from nose to tail and rail to rail. This will minimize drag. Keep the rig over the board for maximum drive but lean out as far as possible and let the rig take your weight. Rake the rig back so that the inefficient gap between the foot of the sail and the board is closed.

Above: two multi-rigged boards, a tandem and a tridem.

Below left: Try and close the 'gap' and keep the board level.

Below right: Two specialist speed boards. Note the narrow shapes.

FREESTYLE

Freestyle is what could be described as the gymnastic branch of windsurfing. Its adherents attempt to perform technically difficult manoeuvres with calculated balance and style. As a windsurfing discipline, freestyle predates funboarding by five or six years. Some people may find it hard to believe these days when the 360-degree loop is commonplace in Hawaii, that the simple rail-ride was once regarded as the most radical manoeuvre the skilled sailor could attempt. It first started with a few sailors experimenting with the boards to see what was possible, but before long it had grown into a boardsailing discipline in its own right, incorporating recognized tricks, routines and competitions. In 1977 (ancient history in windsurfing terms), the International Windsurfer Class incorporated freestyle as an official discipline in its World Championships.

Freestyle reached its peak of popularity in the early 1980s and though it has been eclipsed somewhat by the advent of funboards and high-wind sailing, it remains a favourite of many boardsailors today. Its attractions lie in its simplicity and versatility: all you need is a standard long board, calm water and a little wind. Flat water and light winds are more often than not the conditions encountered by the average boardsailor, especially if he lives inland. Learning the rail-ride or some other trick will frequently prove more appealing than floating around the lake in sub-planing conditions.

Many of today's essential funboard manoeuvres, such as the water start and the flare gybe, started life as freestyle tricks. And many of today's top funboard competitors learned their board-handling skills practising freestyle routines before funboards were invented. Freestyle is

Freestyle is an excellent way of practising your board-handling skills.

FREESTYLE

Dee Caldwell, ex-European Freestyle Champion, demonstrates the classic freestyle trick, the rail-ride.

Top left: Sailing on a reach, Dee hooks his front foot under the windward rail.

Top right: As the rail flips up, Dee places his foot on the daggerboard.

Above left: And puts his back foot onto the rail.

Above right: It is then simply a matter of bringing up his front foot to complete a proper rail-ride.

Right and far right: A head dip and a tail sink, two easy tricks.

still an ideal way to sharpen your windsurfing skills. Many elements of freestyle sailing have subsequently turned up in general funboard techniques. Apart from those already mentioned, sinking the tail, flipping the rig, ducking under the sail and sailing clew-first are all skills required when sailing a funboard.

During a freestyle competition, each competitor is required to sail a routine of three minutes' duration. They may be asked to perform particular tricks or they may be allowed to choose their own. The judges, whose numbers can vary from two to four or more, depending on the size of the event, will evaluate each performance on the style and fluidity of each trick and the routine as a whole, and will also award marks for the number and difficulty of the tricks attempted.

At a more basic level, a mass freestyle is organized where a number of competitors are required to perform a particular trick. Anyone who fails to accomplish it correctly is eliminated. As the tricks get harder and harder, more and more competitors drop out until only the winner remains.

Counting the variations on each basic trick, the number of possible freestyle tricks number in their hundreds. Some are very simple and can be attempted almost as soon as you have learned to sail.

Tricks such as sailing inside the boom, sailing backwards, sailing clew-first, nose and tail sinks, and the head dip should be part of the freestyle sailor's armoury after just a few days' practice.

Other more complicated tricks can be more difficult. These include tricks with such strange names as the clew-first spin, the sail 360 and the everole (which involves sailing the board upside down with the sailor standing on the bottom of the board). The most famous of all freestyle tricks, however, is the rail-ride – sailing the board along on its edge – which can be performed forwards, backwards, to windward or to leeward. Not only that, water starts, duck tacks, splits, head dips and even pirouettes (each of them valid freestyle tricks in themselves) can all be performed 'on the rail'.

When attempting freestyle tricks, avoid heavy winds, choppy waters and boards with footstraps. They will all make life difficult. However, any long stable board without sharp edges will do. A wetsuit will protect your shins from injury. Practise some of the tricks on shore first and when you have learned a few try putting them together in a routine. With a few freestyle tricks under your belt, the next time you venture out on your funboard you should feel much more confident in your own board-handling skills.

Top left: A pirouette: spin around and catch the sail again – easy in a light wind.

Top right: Sailing clew-first: something you will find yourself doing frequently on a funboard.

Opposite top right: A duck tack: instead of walking around the front of the mast, duck under the sail when the board is heading into the wind.

Opposite top far right: A leeward rail-ride: one of the most difficult tricks of all – flipping up the leeward rail and balancing the sail against the wind.

Opposite right: The clew-first water start: another freestyle trick useful for funboard sailing – especially when you fall off halfway through a carve gybe.

Opposite far right: A somersault through the boom: very few sailors can recover from this trick but, when accomplished, it makes an excellent finale to a freestyle routine.

COMPETITIVE WINDSURFING

The world of windsurfing competition is a complex one. Not only are there a number of different racing formulas – each designed to suit different boards and conditions – there are also a number of different racing authorities. Each has its own set of rules (although these often overlap) and each operates local, national and world championships independently of the others.

From top-level international racing down to informal racing at club level, however, windsurfing competition can be divided into two basic types: traditional triangle racing and modern funboard racing. Triangle racing around the world is run under the auspices of the International Yacht Racing Union (IYRU) and its affiliated national sailing authorities in each member country. Funboard competition on the other hand is run on a more commercial basis by the World Sailboard Manufacturers' Association (WSMA). The WSMA was originally formed to promote and develop funboard racing on the type of boards the manufacturers themselves were selling but which were banned from IYRU racing by the latter's bureaucratic measurement rules. At first, the WSMA catered for a professional circuit of its own creation but the racing formats it established have now filtered down to a more grass-roots level.

IYRU racing

In the early days of windsurfing, when the sport was more closely affiliated to traditional sailing than it is today, boardsailors who wanted to race borrowed the event frameworks and competition rules used by conventional sailors. The result was that competitive windsurfing became another branch of yacht racing run by the IYRU.

International Boardsailing Association (IBSA) runs international Division II racing while individual sailing authorities in each of the participating countries run Open Class racing up to national championship level.

One-designs

Some boards and rigs are faster than others and it is sometimes difficult to determine whether it was a sailor's ability or his equipment that helped him to win a particular race. Large numbers of competitive sailors therefore prefer to race in one-design classes, in which competitors race on identical boards.

There are many one-design classes. Some are more popular than others, but only three are recognized by the IYRU as international racing classes. These are the International Windsurfer Class Association (IWCA), the International Windglider Class (IWGC) and the International Mistral Class Organization (IMCO). The first of these, the IWCA, was once the largest sailboard class of all and is certainly the oldest, having been formed at the beginning of the seventies and not long after the invention of the Windsurfer itself. The Class still uses an updated version of Hoyle Schweitzer's original Windsurfer.

The Windglider, the board used by the IWGC, was chosen by the IYRU as the

Opposite left: IMCO: one of the most popular one-design racing classes.

Above: Open Class Division II triangle racing: note the rounded displacement hulls designed for fast upwind sailing.

In order to standardize racing around the world, the IYRU recognized three international one-design classes and in 1980 organized 'open-class' racing into three divisions: Division I for standard flatboards, Division II for 'round' or displacement boards, and Division III for tandems. Although boards of any brand could be used in Open Class racing, measurement rules were introduced to keep competition on a reasonably equal basis. This particularly applied to Division I which was seen as the class for mass-participation racing at club and local level, and so no world championships were planned. Division II, however, was seen as the development class catering for top-level international competition on the fastest boards available – at the time these were the displacement boards specifically designed for triangle racing. In light-to-medium winds they are still the fastest boards on flat water. Today the

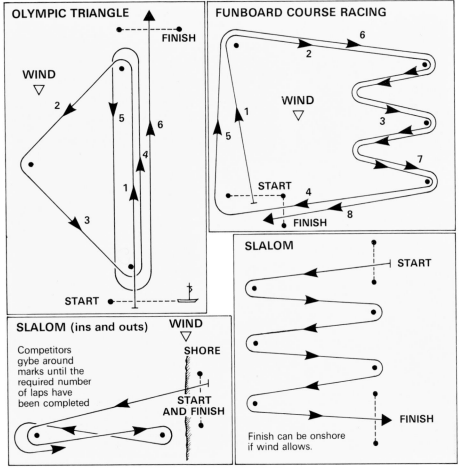

Triangle racing

The one-design classes and each of the Open Class divisions use the triangle-racing format and IYRU racing rules. The Olympic triangle is the most common course used – competitors race around three marks – completing three windward legs, two reaching legs and a downwind leg, or what is known as a 'triangle-sausage-beat' configuration (the 'sausage' being a windward leg followed by a downwind leg. With three windward legs the emphasis is on beating and this is where the sailors' racing and tactical abilities really come into play.

Triangle-racing rules are complicated but are primarily concerned with rights of way and course infringements (touching a mark or prematurely crossing the start line). If a sailor infringes a rule he is obliged to perform a 720-degree penalty turn (turning the board through 360 degrees twice) to absolve himself or, in the cases of touching a mark, sail around it again giving way to everybody else.

Of course, many sailors will try to get away with rule infringements, in which case they can be 'protested' by either the race committee or a fellow sailor (who must shout '720' or 'protest' at the time of the infringement. Protests are heard after the race by a protest committee which, after examining the evidence of witnesses, will rule one way or the other. A successful protest usually results in the disqualification of the guilty sailor.

One rule that often produces protests at sailboard regattas is IYRU Rule 54 which outlaws 'pumping' (a rapid in-out movement of the rig to gain headway). It is a difficult rule to police as well as being tempting to indulge in and is dropped in all other forms of sailboard racing. Because of the complicated structure of triangle-racing rules, races can often be won off the water by sailors who have in-

depth knowledge of the rules and experience of protest committees and know how to use both to their advantage.

Protests aside, competitors are awarded points according to their finishing positions in a particular race. For example, first place will score 0 points, second place 3 points, third place 5.7 points, fourth place 8 points and so on. Other scoring systems will begin with 0.7 points for the winner with second place getting 2 points, third place 3 points etc. During a series of races, or a regatta, a number of races will be held and each competitor will be allowed to discard his worst result. For example, the best five out of his six results will count. The sailor with the lowest overall score will win the regatta. Frequently, the fleet will be divided up into weight categories, generally light and heavyweight, with separate fleets for youths, seniors and ladies.

Funboard racing

Whereas triangle racing has been borrowed from other forms of sailing, funboard racing formats have been specifically designed to cater for modern sailboards. The WSMA was the first to compile and publish a set of rules and these were first put together for the World Funboard Cup series of 1983 and 1984. The WSMA recognizes three different funboard disciplines: course racing, slalom and wave performance.

Funboard course racing is a modified form of traditional triangle racing but with less upwind sailing and a much more relaxed set of rules. As the WSMA states as a basic principle in its rule book: 'These [course-racing] rules are intended to ensure that the best competitor wins through skill, good fortune and quality of equipment alone and not as a result of procedural devices or legalistic argument.' Consequently, funboards race around 'flattened' triangles under IYRU rules from which the less appropriate rules have been deleted.

Slalom racing is intended to cater for shorter boards that are primarily designed for fast reaching and gybing. There are many different types of slalom course, but none of them involve tacking or difficult upwind or downwind sailing. Ideally, slalom competitions are held in side-shore winds around two buoys positioned close to shore and in surf conditions if possible. Heats of competitors set out from the beach, reach between the two marks and gybe around each of them three or four times in a figure-of-eight course before returning to the beach. Some slalom courses start off-shore and competitors sail a zig-zag course around a number of gybe-marks.

Slalom competitions generally require

Top: Funboard course racing: top professionals never race in less than 15 knots of wind and use courses with the minimum of upwind work.

Above: Slalom racing: competitors race in heats of between two and eight sailors. Courses are set in and out of surf if possible.

official sailboard for Windsurfing's first Olympic Games in Los Angeles in 1984. Even then, the Windglider was outdated and now that Division II has been chosen as the official Olympic class, the fortunes of the IWGC have faded somewhat.

IMCO is the most recent of the international one-designs classes (being formed in 1978) but with one of the fastest and most modern boards, the Mistral Superlight, it is one of the most popular.

minutes. Again, very few rules are involved.

Both slalom and wave-performance competitions use either single or double-elimination ladders to determine an eventual winner. The single-elimination system is similar to a straight knock-out contest but double elimination allows the losers of the early heats a second chance (although a second loss means elimination from the contest).

Speed sailing

Most forms of windsurfing competition set sailors against each other but speed sailing pits the sailor against the clock. Equipment and sailing techniques have developed rapidly over recent years with the result that the sailboard speed record has nearly doubled in less than ten years from the 17.1 knots set by a Dutchman, called Derk Thijs, in 1977 to the 32.35 knots achieved by the Austrian Michael Pucher in 1985.

Speed sailing is a specialist branch of windsurfing and requires very special conditions – a Force 8 or even a Force 9 gale and flat calm water, conditions that occur simultaneously only in certain parts of the world. Weymouth in England, Port St. Louis-du-Rhône in France and Fremantle in Australia are three well-known speed-sailing venues.

Left: Wave performance: pairs of sailors display their skill at wave riding, wave jumping and transitions in front of a panel of judges.

Below: Speed sailing: using sophisticated rigs and very small boards to minimize drag, sailors race against the clock over a 500-m (546-yd) course.

a minimum windspeed of around Force 4 or more (the WSMA stipulates a minimum of 15 knots). Although one slalom competitor can 'protest' another, most race organizers use only a basic set of rules designed to avoid collisions.

A wave-riding and jumping contest is probably the most dramatic of all forms of windsurfing competition. Unfortunately, it is also the rarest as suitable conditions are hard to come by. Nevertheless, given a minimum of a Force 4 wind and the smallest of waves, top windsurfing professionals can put on startling displays of windsurfing with routines that can include 360-degree barrel rolls, aerial off-the-lips and 180-degree bottom turns. During WSMA wave-performance events, competitors sail in pairs and are marked by a panel of judges on their wave riding, wave jumping gybing etc., over a period of between five and twelve

Racing Tactics and Technique

There is a great deal more to serious sailboard racing than simply attempting to sail around the course as fast as you can. Good board speed is important, of course, and must be practised until you can sail at maximum efficiency on all points of sailing without thinking, but your eventual place on the results list will depend on many other factors. These include your mental and physical preparation, your choice of equipment, your tactical ability and your awareness of rules and procedures. These can all combine to give you a slight edge over your competitors or, if you haven't paid attention to them, they could result in a position well down the fleet.

At nearly all regattas and race meetings the race officer will give the competitors a briefing. It is worth paying attention to this, as he will describe the courses and starting signals to be used, any special rules that will apply, and any changes that might have been made to the published sailing instructions (which you should have studied carefully already). A thorough knowledge of the rules and the format of the day's events, whether it be triangle racing, slalom or wave-riding, will help you to maintain the correct mental attitude, secure in the knowledge that every possible preparation has been

made. Most top sailors put their success down to concentration and you can concentrate on the job in hand only if you know exactly what to do in every situation.

Preparation for a race can start hours before you reach the start line. Make sure you have chosen the correct size of sail for what you expect the conditions to be and ensure that the board is rigged and tuned properly. If you are sailing in a restricted class, make sure your equipment fits the measurement rules. Make yourself a checklist of questions to be answered

Top: A line start seconds after the gun.

Above: A Le Mans beach start for a slalom race.

Opposite: Your tactics around the course should be dictated by wind and water conditions. On the beats, it is important to remember when taking advantage of the windshifts that starboard tack (right-hand forward on the boom) has right of way over port tack (left-hand forward on the boom).

before you set out for the start line: Is your daggerboard correctly adjusted? Will your mast track operate freely? Is your hull smooth and is there sufficient non-slip on the deck? Are you sure your harness lines are not frayed and are they set at the correct length? Is your boom at the correct height and is there enough fullness in the sail for the conditions?

Research before the race can pay dividends later. Find out what the weather forecast is. If the wind strength is likely to increase, for example, let this influence your choice of sail, or if you are sailing in a restricted class, set your sail flat to allow for the stronger winds. Knowledge that the wind's direction is likely to change will give you a tactical advantage later in the race.

If you are racing on a river estuary or the sea, investigate the tides and currents. You can use these to your advantage during the race – especially in light winds.

Aim to arrive on the course early. This will allow you to warm up and get used to the conditions. It will also give you an opportunity to inspect the course and its peculiarities so that you can formulate a strategy for the race itself. Successful tactical racing is very much a question of judging the situation correctly and taking action accordingly. The more facts you have at your fingertips on wind directions, start-line biases, wind bends, wind shadows, tides and currents, the better your decision-making will be after the start.

Basic tactics

The tactical possibilities in sailboard racing are almost endless and there are few sports in which tactics play such an important role. The knowledge and use of basic tactics are essential if you want to be at the front of the fleet, as few races are won on board speed alone. Slalom is the only real exception to this but even slalom, which is expressly designed to test a competitor's sailing ability, rather than his tactical ability, does contain an element of tactical racing (using your wind shadow, adopting the optimum line around a mark etc.).

In all forms of course racing (triangle and funboard), the race officer will have to lay the course according to the wind direction. In theory, the first mark (the windward mark) should be placed directly upwind of the start line so that the start line is at right angles to the wind. However, as the wind never blows continuously from the same direction, and because positioning a set of buoys in moving water with pin-point accuracy is an impossible task, one end of the start line will be closer to the wind than the other. And if the mark itself is not directly

upwind of the start, you will be able to sail at a better angle towards it on one tack than on the other.

The wind itself is always shifting – either from side to side like a pendulum or constantly in one direction. If you are sailing upwind you will either be 'lifted' and so find yourself able to sail a more direct course to the mark; or you will be 'headed' so that you have to bear off a bit in order to prevent luffing and then tack to take advantage of the shift.

'Clean' wind over a course is rare and obstacles near the course – such as rocky headlands, islands, clumps of trees, tall buildings etc. – will influence its flow, producing wind shadows and wind bends. Obviously, steering clear of wind shadows is a good idea (an obstacle can disrupt the wind for a distance downwind twenty or even thirty times its own height) but wind bends can be used to your advantage. The wind will bend in an arc around an obstacle such as a headland. Sailing into its centre so that you are lifted both on your way in and on your way out will give you an advantage over someone on an unaffected part of the course.

Your speed from A to B is your speed through the water. If the water itself is moving, then your speed will be affected. Because water is slowed by contact with land, it can pay to be in shallower water – generally nearer the shore – when you are sailing against the tide. A 1-knot reduction in the flow against you is a 1-knot increase in speed. The reverse is true if you are sailing with the current when it is obviously an advantage to be in the area where it is flowing at its fastest. Tides change, so don't make the mistake of assuming the best strategy on the first leg will be the best on a subsequent one. It can even be worth programming the alarm on your watch to warn you of a tide change.

Choosing the optimum route over the course is always a compromise, as all the above variables have to be considered. Some will complement each other and some will cancel each other out. It is no use sailing to the inshore side of the course to take advantage of a 1-knot reduction in an adverse current when further out to sea the wind is blowing 2 or 3 knots faster. Again, careful study of the course and the conditions beforehand will pay off during the race.

The fact that the smooth flow of wind is disturbed by obstacles means that you can use your own rig as a weapon. As the wind flows over the sail, an area of 'dirty' wind is created downwind of the sail. Not only must you avoid being 'blanketed' or covered by an opponent, you should use your own wind shadow to slow down another competitor.

The exact size and position of your sail's wind shadow will vary according to the wind strength (the lighter the wind, the greater the disruption) and your direction of sailing. Running downwind and reaching create large wind shadows downwind of the sail, but a close-hauled sail creates a shadow that moves aft in relation to the board as the wind strength increases. Also, because of the way air flows over the sail, boards slightly behind and to *windward* will suffer from the 'lee-bow' effect. This occurs when the wind is deflected from the windward side of the leading sail onto the leeward side of the sail slightly behind and to windward. This will cause the following board to slow down and drop back.

Using the right-of-way rules to cover an opponent and possibly force him to tack, lose speed and even miss a mark is also a valid racing tactic. There are many possibilities – far too many to go into here, but the following example illustrates the potential for attacking a single opponent. If you are sailing on a starboard tack (on which you have right of way) and you meet your victim on port, you can sail across his bows and tack so that you are covering him. If put in this situation yourself, tack back across your opponent's stern as quickly as possible. He will then be forced to tack again to maintain his cover, but two tacks in a row may slow him down considerably and you will be able to escape. Beware, however, of battling with individual competitors and allowing the rest of the fleet to pass you by.

Tactical racing is therefore a question of manoeuvring your immediate opponents into zones of dirty wind while keeping out of them yourself, and at the same time following a broader strategy that exploits the conditions on the course as a whole.

Line starts and gate starts

Triangle racing employs either the standard line start or a gate start. In theory, the gate start gives every competitor an equal chance on the start line. A pathfinder, chosen from the fleet, sails on a close-hauled port tack across the front of the fleet and is followed close behind by a gate boat. The rest of the fleet then sails behind the gate boat and across the imaginary line the pathfinder has just made. Even if you are the last to cross the line you will be at no real disadvantage because the pathfinder will, in effect, have sailed your first tack for you.

The line start is the most commonly used in triangle racing and can involve a good deal of jostling for position amongst competitors. Unless the line has been laid perfectly (in which case you should start in the middle) it will be biased to port or to starboard. To discover the bias, simply stop on the line with the sail luffing down the centerline of the board. Whichever end of the line the nose of your board tends to point to will be the favoured end.

Although starting at the favoured end will have benefits, there are other considerations to take into account: the number of other sailors with the same intention, your ability to get to the best position without infringing anyone's rights of way, and your intended course after the start itself. This is where your knowledge of the rights-of-way rules and your close-quarter manoeuvring skills will come into play.

It is also worth taking a transit so that you know exactly where the line is. Taking a transit involves lining up the two marks (one may be the committee boat), indicating each end of the line with an object such as a tree or a flag pole on the shore. When the race starts you merely have to line up one of the marks with the transit on shore to judge where the line is. With other marks and transits this technique can be used to judge your position on the course at other times during the race.

The starting procedure is governed by

a number of signals, the timing of which varies between International Yacht Racing Union racing, which requires five-minute intervals, and World Sailboard Manufacturers' Association funboard racing, which specifies three-minute intervals. These are:
i) warning signal
ii) preparatory signal
iii) starting signal.
The signal itself is generally a gun accompanied by a visual signal. The WSMA uses a traffic-light system (red, yellow and green flags) while the IYRU rules specify the use of the class flag or a white shape for the warning signal; the 'blue peter' flag for the preparatory signal and a red flag, or the lowering of the first two, for the starting signal. (Other signals may be given at the start and during the race. Consult the relevant rule book for the details.)

Le Mans starts

In some forms of racing, such as slalom and long-distance, a Le Mans style beach start is used. Competitors line up on the beach and when the signal is given (a red, a yellow and then a green flag at one- or three-minute intervals in WSMA racing) they run to the water's edge carrying or pushing their boards ahead of them and

Above: A useful racing tactic is 'blanketing' an opponent's wind. However, remember that an overtaking board and a board to windward (in this case No. 46) must keep clear.

Opposite: Mark-rounding in course racing: within two board lengths of a mark, a board on the inside has right of way over boards on the outside if the inside board has an overlap. On the other hand, if there is no overlap when the leading board comes within two board lengths of the mark, then the board behind (inside or not) must keep clear until both have rounded the mark.

then beach start in the normal way.

Position on the line is not as crucial as it is on a line start because the wind will normally be cross-shore. In small slalom heats, position on the line is often allocated. But in larger fleets, it is a matter of jostling for position. Starting at either end of the line (if possible the upwind end) is preferable to being caught in the mêlée of boards in the middle.

Frequently, a beach finish will follow a beach start. This involves sailing as close

Right: Different types of start.

Far right: How boards are affected by another's dirty wind:
A is suffering from the lee-bow effect
B is headed by deflected and turbulent wind
C is in a wind shadow.

Below and below right: How to use wind bends and wind shifts to your advantage.

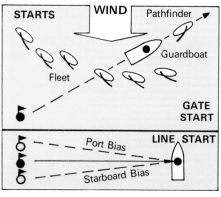

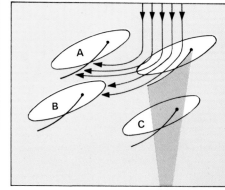

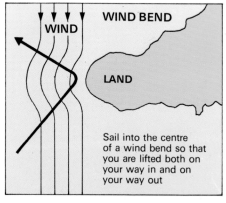

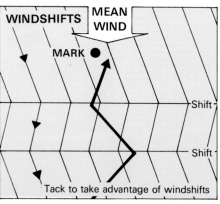

to the shore as you can (without risking too much damage to your board and skeg) and then running the last few yards up the beach to a finish line between two flags.

Around the course

In traditional triangle racing, tactics come into play mainly on the start line and the beats; races are often won on the first beat alone. Subsequent legs do present opportunities, however. Reaching legs are more a matter of board speed but the line you take to the gybe mark and then to the leeward mark will not necessarily be straight. Consider the vagaries of the wind and tides, the opportunities for covering an opponent (but avoid being covered yourself) and the preferred position when you reach the marks (the inside is usually the best – the right-of-way rules are normally on your side).

Running downwind is probably the most peculiar leg. Those behind have the unique opportunity of spoiling the wind of the leaders, who are unable to respond. It is sometimes better to sail a series of broad reaches, taking advantage of any waves that are travelling in the same direction, instead of sailing a slow and unstable course directly downwind.

Finish lines can be as biased as start lines and if you can detect the direction of the bias, it will obviously be an advantage to sail on the tack that takes you over the downwind end of the line first.

Funboard racing tactics

Because minimum windspeeds (usually 12 or 15 knots) are required in funboard racing and because the course is a 'flattened' triangle, gear selection (e.g. sail size) and board speed become considerably more important than in triangle racing. Nevertheless, it is important to consider tactics carefully. Although the beats are short and over quickly, taking the wrong line and having to tack too often will lose valuable time. Everything happens much faster during a funboard race, so mistakes, such as falling off at a mark, will cost you dearly.

SAFETY FACTORS

Winds and Weather

The weather influences the strength and direction of the wind. The ability to interpret forecasts and recognize the changing state of the weather will help you to avoid problems and find the right conditions in which to sail.

Wind is created by differences in atmospheric pressure between areas of high pressure (highs or anticyclones) and low pressure (lows or depressions). These are indicated on weather maps by isobars which connect areas of equal pressure at intervals of five millibars. Due to the differences in pressure, air tends to flow from highs to lows, but because of the earth's rotation, the air actually spirals out of highs and into lows. The steeper the pressure gradient is (i.e. the closer the isobars are together), the stronger the wind will be. Generally speaking, the wind will follow the direction of the isobars. This will be anticlockwise around lows and clockwise around highs in the northern hemisphere and the reverse in the southern hemisphere.

Above: Always examine the weather forecast before sailing.

Below: Know the times of the tide and beware of adverse currents.

Highs move slowly and are associated with calm, settled weather and light winds. Lows move much faster and, because they absorb warm air from tropical regions and cold air from polar regions, they develop warm and cold fronts which can bring stronger winds and rain.

Other local factors also affect the wind's strength and direction. Wind will bend around obstacles such as mountains and will speed up as it is tunnelled down valleys. The fierce Mistral wind in the south of France is a good example of this. However, the most common local phenomenon is the sea breeze. During the day as the sun heats up the air over land and it begins to rise, it is replaced by cool air from the sea, producing an onshore sea breeze. Because the sea cools more slowly than the land, the situation is reversed during the night and the air flows back out to sea, producing an offshore wind. Remember to take local conditions into account when checking the forecast.

Above: Never sail alone and always tell someone ashore where you are going.

Right: Beware of strong winds.

Tides and currents

Tides go up and down under the influence of the moon's gravitational pull every six hours or so. It is useful to know the times of the tide not just because you will need to know if there will be enough water in which to sail, but also because a changing tide can produce strong irregular currents, especially in shallow, offshore waters. Tide tables are published for most localities but asking local sailors is the only sure way of finding out about any unusually strong currents which could prove to be dangerous.

Seamanship and the rules of the road

Although the ocean may seem to be a vast open space, collisions between different craft can and do occur. There is an internationally recognized set of 'rules of the road' which you should know before setting sail. If you find yourself about to collide with a powered vessel, the rule that normally applies is 'sail has right of way over power'. Use your common sense, however; don't argue with oil tankers and give way to larger vessels and yachts in navigation channels where there is a danger of them running aground.

As you shouldn't be windsurfing in shipping lanes, problems are more likely to arise when you meet smaller sailing craft or other boards. Three basic rules apply here:

1 Starboard tack has right of way over port tack (i.e. if the wind is blowing over your port side you must give way).

2 When two boards are on the same tack, the windward board must keep clear.

THE BEAUFORT SCALE OF WIND FORCE

Wind Force	Wind Speed (knots)	Description	Effects on the sea	Probable wave height (metres)	Effect on land
0	0–1	Calm	Sea like a mirror.	0	Smoke rises vertically.
1	1–3	Light air	Ripples with the appearance of scales are formed, but without foam crests.	0.1	Direction of wind shown by smoke but not by wind vanes.
2	4–6	Light breeze	Small wavelets, still short but more pronounced. Crests have a glassy appearance and do not break.	0.5	Leaves rustle, wind vane moves with the wind.
3	7–10	Gentle breeze	Large wavelets. Crests begin to break. Foam of glassy appearance. Perhaps scattered white horses.	1.0	Continual motion of leaves and small twigs.
4	11–16	Moderate breeze	Small waves, becoming longer, fairly frequent white horses.	2.0	Small branches move. Raises dust and loose paper.
5	17–21	Fresh breeze	Moderate waves, taking a more pronounced long form, many white horses are formed. Chance of some spray.	3.0	Small trees sway, crest wavelets on inland waters.
6	22–27	Strong breeze	Large waves begin to form, the white foam crests are more extensive everywhere. Probably some spray.	4.0	Large branches move, telegraph wires 'whistle', umbrellas used with difficulty.
7	28–33	Near gale	Sea heaps up and white foam from breaking waves begin to be blown in streaks along the direction of the wind.		Whole trees sway, inconvenient to walk against the wind.
8	34–40	Gale	Moderately high waves of greater length, edges of crests begin to break into spindrift. The foam is blown in well-marked streaks.		Breaks twigs off trees, wind generally impedes progress.
9	41–47	Strong gale	High waves. Dense streaks of foam along the direction of the wind. Crests of waves begin to topple, tumble and roll over. Spray may affect visibility.	7.0	Slight structural damage occurs (e.g. chimney pots and roof slates blown away).
10	48–55	Storm	Very high waves with long overhanging crests. The resulting foam in great patches is blown in dense white streaks along the direction of the wind. The surface of the sea takes on a white appearance. The tumbling of the sea becomes heavy and shocklike. Visability affected.	9.0	Trees uprooted, considerable structural damage occurs.

The Beaufort Scale of wind force is more than the mere categorization of windspeeds. It is also a scale which relates the wind force to the behaviour of the sea. The speed of the wind can be estimated from the behaviour of the sea, or vice-versa. The effects of the wind on land have been included to help you assess the conditions before venturing out onto the sea.

The scale is designed for the open sea so the effects may vary in enclosed waters or near land with an offshore wind. This is particularly true of the wave heights which will be smaller but steeper.

Below: Self-help. If you find yourself unable to sail back to shore, either because of equipment breakage, too much wind or even too little wind, it is of the utmost importance that you know how to practise self-rescue: sit on the board facing the wind; detach the rig, remove any battens, and roll up the sail as tightly as possible. Without removing the inhaul, place the boom parallel to the mast, lashing the sail to the mast with the uphaul and the outhaul. Place the rig along the length of the board; kneel on either side of it (or lie on top of it in rough water) and paddle back to shore. If you have problems, ditch the rig but never leave the board.

Above: The internationally recognized distress signal is to slowly wave your arms back and forth above your head. Setting off a flare or waving a fluorescent orange (dayglo) flag will also help to attract attention.

3 An overtaking vessel must keep clear. (This applies to all craft, powered or otherwise.)

The above rules should always be tempered with common sense. Take decisive action yourself, but don't assume the other party will know the rules or what he is supposed to do.

On certain waters, windsurfing may be restricted to particular areas or prohibited altogether. Take notice of these rules and be courteous to other water users for the good name of the sport.

Ten safety rules

Windsurfing is normally a safe sport but you could find yourself in trouble if you don't observe all the following safety rules:

1 *Always check the weather forecast and times of tide changes.* This will help you to avoid being caught out in strong winds, bad weather or adverse currents.

2 *Don't overestimate your own abilities.* Give safety the benefit of the doubt: use a smaller sized sail and don't venture out in conditions you may be unable to handle. Don't go out too far too soon.

3 *Never sail in an offshore wind* unless you are an experienced sailor and help is close at hand. Offshore winds will always be stronger a short distance out to sea.

4 *Wear sufficient protection.* Even in warm weather a wet body will be cooled rapidly by the wind. In cold weather, an efficient wetsuit or drysuit is necessary if you are to avoid hypothermia.

5 *Examine your equipment thoroughly.* Sailboard equipment rarely fails at sea, but if

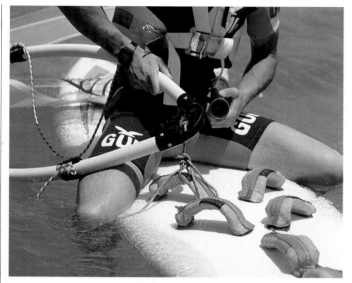

Above: If you have a fully battened sail and you want to self-rescue, don't remove the battens (a very difficult procedure at sea) but detach the boom and remove the sail from the mast instead. Roll up the sail and, if you can, use the mast as a paddle.

it does you could be in serious trouble. In particular, check the mast foot for wear and replace any frayed lines. Always use a rig safety leash and carry distress flares and a spare length of rope.

6 *Choose your sailing area with care.* Avoid vicious shorebreaks, strong currents, and rocky shorelines where your return to shore will be restricted. Don't sail in shipping lanes or near swimmers.

7 *Never sail alone.* Always sail in pairs or in groups. Tell someone on shore where you are going and when you expect to be back. They will then be able to raise the alarm if necessary.

8 *Learn to recognize the onset of hypothermia.* The symptoms of hypothermia (where the body's core temperature drops below its usual 98.4°F (37°C) can develop

rapidly if the sailor is suddenly immersed in extremely cold water, or they can creep up insidiously after repeated immersions and exposure to wind chill. Uncontrolled shivering and disorientation at 95°F (35°C) are followed by a sense of well-being and amnesia at 91.4°F (33°C), irregular heart beat and semi-consciousness at 86°F (30°C) and then total unconsciousness and death. If you feel the initial symptoms coming on, return to shore immediately and warm yourself under a hot shower, or with warm blankets or by some other means. Anyone else suffering from hypothermia must be removed from the water and warmed up as soon as possible. Give mouth-to-mouth resuscitation if necessary and, except in mild cases, seek medical help.

9 *Never leave your board.* Sailboards never sink and make ideal life-rafts.

10 *Learn the distress signals and self-help techniques.* They are illustrated on these pages. Practise them before a real emergency occurs. One day you may be glad you did.

Above: Always use a safety leash to prevent loss of the rig at sea (this one plugs into the spare mast well) and regularly check the universal joint and mast foot for wear and tear.

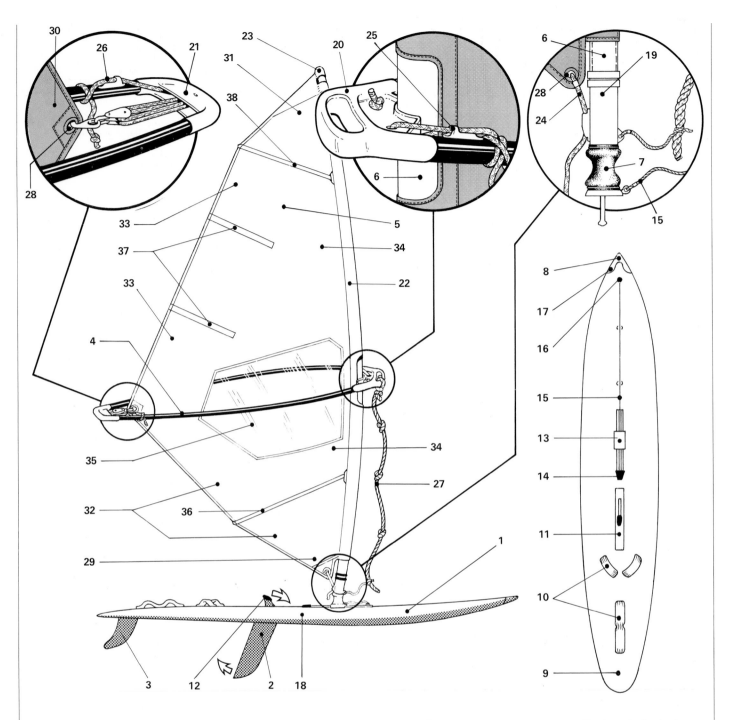

Parts of a Sailboard

No two boards are identical and will vary according to brand and type. Common to all boards are six of the seven basic constituent parts: the hull, the skeg, the sail, the mast, the boom and the universal joint. The seventh constituent part, the daggerboard, is only fitted to boards longer than 3m (10ft) or so. Other specifications also vary from board to board. For example, a particular board may have two mast 'wells' instead of a mast track; it may have no footstraps fitted; and the sail may have a number of full-length battens or it may have no battens at all. However, the illustration above includes most of the parts you are likely to find on a modern funboard.

1 The board or hull
2 Daggerboard
3 Skeg (or fin)
4 Boom (wishbone)
5 Sail
6 Mast
7 Mast foot and
   universal joint (UJ)
8 Nose (bow)
9 Tail (stern)
10 Footstraps
11 Daggerboard slot
12 Daggerboard handle
13 Mast track
14 Mast-track pedal
15 Safety leash

16 Towing eye
17 Nose bumper
18 Rails
   (edges of the board)
19 Mast extension
20 Boom end (front)
21 Boom end (clew)
22 Luff (mast) sleeve
23 Mast head
24 Downhaul rope and
   cleat (sometimes fitted
   with a pulley system)
25 Inhaul and cleat
26 Outhaul and cleat
27 Uphaul (with
   shock cord fitted)

28 Eyelets (cringles)
   for rigging purposes
29 Tack of sail
30 Clew of sail
31 Head of sail
32 Foot of sail
33 Leech of sail
34 Luff of sail
35 Sail window
36 Foot batten (full
   length) contained in
   batten pocket
37 Leech battens (short)
38 Head batten
   (full length)

90

GLOSSARY

Abeam To the side of the board.
ABS A plastic skin material.
Apparent wind A combination of the true wind and the wind induced by the movement of the board.
ASA Similar to ABS.
Aspect ratio The ratio of mast height to boom length, e.g. a high aspect sail has a tall, thin profile.
Asymmetric board A board with one half of the tail the optimal shape for bottom turns and the other half for cutbacks.
Battens Strips of plastic or glass fibre used to support and stabilize the sail.
Beam reach The point of sailing 90 degrees to the wind.
Beating Sailing upwind as close to the wind as possible.
Bear off/away To turn away from the wind.
Beaufort scale A system for classifying wind speeds.
Blank A block of polyurethane or polystyrene foam from which a custom board is shaped.
Blindstitching A wetsuit stitch that doesn't pierce the material.
Boardsailing An alternative term for windsurfing.
Bottom turn A fast turn made at the bottom of a wave.
Bowline A knot often used on the downhaul.
Break An area offshore where waves are breaking.
Broad reach The fastest point of sailing, approximately 135 degrees off the wind.
Camber The amount of curve in a sail.
Camber inducer A plastic device in the luff sleeve designed to induce extra camber in the sail.
Cavitation The situation where aerated water flows down the skeg, eventually causing it to lose its grip and 'spin-out'.
Centre of effort (CE) The point on the sail representing the sum of all the forces acting upon it. Usually close to the point of maximum camber (draught).
Centre of lateral resistance (CLR) A point representing the sum of all the forces of resistance offered by the board and around which the board pivots. (In practice this is the daggerboard.)
Cleat A fitting for securing ropes.
Clew The outermost corner of the sail.
Clew-first Sailing with the clew pointing towards the wind and with the airflow reversed over the sail.
Close-hauled Sailing close to the wind with the sail as close to the centreline of the board as possible.
Close reach The point of sailing between a beat and a beam reach.
Concaves Speed-enhancing hollow grooves on the underside of the hull.
Cringles Small metal eyelets used on the tack and clew.
Critical section The part of a wave that has just begun to break.
Custom board ('customs') A one-off, hand-shaped and laminated board.
Cutback A sharp turn near the top of a wave back down its face.
Dacron A trade name for polyester cloth.

Ding A small hole or dent in a (particularly custom) board.
Displacement board A high-volume board with a rounded or 'V'-shape hull.
Displacement sailing Sailing in sub-planing conditions.
Divisions I, II, and III IYRU Open Class racing divisions for flatboards (I), displacement boards (II) and tandems (III).
Downhaul line Attaches the tack of the sail to the mast foot and puts tension in the luff of the sail.
Draught The point of maximum camber in a sail.
Drysuit A totally waterproof suit for cold-weather sailing.
Duck gybe A gybe in which the rig is passed over the sailor's head rather than around the front of the board.
Duck tack A tack in which the sailor ducks under the rig rather than walk around the front of the board.
Epoxy resin A tough plastic laminating resin used in board manufacture.
Eye of the wind The exact direction from which the wind is coming.
Fine reach A point of sailing fractionally off a beat.
Flare gybe A method of gybing a long board by sinking the tail and leeward rail.
Flat sail A sail set with minimum camber for maximum control.
Floater A board that will support the weight of the rig and the sailor when stationary.
Foot (of sail) The bottom edge.
Footsteering Banking the board to one side or another in order to steer it.
Footstraps Straps that hold the sailor's feet on the board in strong winds.
Free-sailing A method of sailing patented by Hoyle Schweitzer which utilizes a universal joint at the base of the mast and a wishbone (two-sided) boom.
Freestyle sailing Performing tricks on a board.
Full sail A sail set with a deep camber for maximum power.
Fully battened sail A sail with full-length battens running from the luff sleeve to the leech and sometimes the foot.
Funboard A term loosely describing a board that performs well in a Force 4 plus wind.
Gel coat The final protective coat on a GRP board.
Glass fibre Glass-fibre matting is used with a plastic resin in the construction of boards, especially 'customs'.
GRP Glass-reinforced plastic.
Gun A board designed for speed.
Gybing Turning the board so that the tail passes through the eye of the wind.
Head (of sail) Top of the sail.
Head up Turn towards the wind.
High aspect See aspect ratio.
Hooked in Sailing with the harness attached to the harness line.
Hull The board itself.
Hypothermia A dangerous medical condition brought on by a drop in the body's core temperature below 37°C (98.4°F).

Inhaul line Secures the boom to the mast.
Ins-and-outs A form of slalom racing in and out of surf.
IYRU International Yacht Racing Union.
Kevlar A stronger, tougher but expensive alternative to glass fibre.
Knots Nautical miles per hour (10 knots is approx. 11.5 mph).
Laminating Attaching one layer of material to another, e.g. laminating glass fibre to a foam blank.
Leech The trailing edge of the sail running from head to clew.
Le Mans start A running start from the beach.
Lee-shore A shoreline downwind (to leeward) of the sailor.
Leeward The direction towards which the wind is blowing, e.g. the side of the board opposite the side over which the wind is blowing.
Leeway Drift to leeward while sailing.
Lip The crest of a wave as it begins to break.
Luffing Allowing the sail to flutter in the wind.
Luff perpendicular The distance between the clew and the boom cut-out on the sail.
Luff sleeve The pocket on one edge of the sail into which the mast is inserted.
Marginal A smallish sail or a board that only just supports the sailor and the rig.
Mast extension Used at the base of the mast to increase or decrease its height.
Mast foot The device that incorporates the universal joint and connects the mast to the board.
Mast sleeve See luff sleeve.
Mast step A hole on the board into which the mast is inserted.
Mast track Used instead of a mast step, it allows the position of the mast to be adjusted back and forth.
Mylar A trade name for a low-stretch polyester film used as a sail material.
Neoprene A closed-cell foam rubber material used in wetsuits.
Non-slip A rough finish on the deck of a board.
Offshore wind A wind blowing away from the shore, which should be avoided by beginners.
Off-the-lip A cutback turn using the lip to knock the board back down the wave.
One-design racing Competition for boards of the same brand and model.
Open-class racing Competition for boards of different brands in a particular class (e.g. IYRU Divisions I and II).
Outhaul line Attaches the clew to the far end of the boom.
Planing Sailing at high speed with minimal water displacement.
Polyester cloth Standard sail material.
Polyester resin The standard resin used with glass fibre.
Polyethylene A tough plastic used as a skin material.
Polystyrene/polyurethane foam Both are used as core material.
Pop-out A short-run GRP board that 'pops out' of a mould.
Port The left-hand side when facing forward on a board.
Powerhead (or Fathead) A standard sail with one or two head battens only.

Power-joint An hour-glass-shaped rubber universal joint.
Pumping The action of pulling the rig in and out, designed to increase speed.
RAF Rotating asymmetrical foil (see rotational sail).
Railing A tipping up of the board caused by mast-foot pressure and a hydroplaning daggerboard.
Rail-riding Sailing the board on its edge.
Rails The sides of the board.
Reaching Sailing across the wind (see broad, beam, close and fine reaching).
Regatta A competitive event consisting of a series of races.
Resin A substance used to impregnate glass-fibre matting etc., which then cures (hardens).
Rig The mast, sail and boom.
Rip A fast-moving tide or current.
Roach The sail area beyond a straight line from head to clew.
Rocker The amount of curvature in a board from nose to tail.
Rotational sail A sail in which the battens 'rotate' from one side of the mast to the other forming an asymmetrical foil shape on either tack.
Roundboard A displacement board.
Running Sailing directly downwind.
Scrim A net-like fabric used to lend tear resistance to Mylar.
Set (a sail) To rig and tune a sail.
Sheeting in/out Adjusting the trim of the sail for more or less power.
Shorebreak Waves breaking on the beach.
Sinker A low-volume board that sinks under the weight of the sailor and rig unless planing.
Skeg (or fin) A small fin near the tail of the board providing directional stability.
Slalom A reaching and gybing course for high-speed racing.
Smoothskin Unlined neoprene.
Spin-out A loss of traction by the skeg caused by cavitation.
Starboard The right-hand side when facing forward on a board.
Steamer A wetsuit designed for minimal water circulation.
Tack (of sail) The bottom corner.
Tacking Sailing a zig-zag course upwind, or turning the board so that the nose passes through the eye of the wind.
Tandem A two-man board.
Tridem A three-man board.
True wind The wind experienced by a stationary individual.
Universal joint A device that allows the rig to be inclined by 180 degrees and rotated through 360 degrees.
Uphaul A rope attached to the front end of the boom and used to pull the rig out of the water.
Vee A hull shape similar to a flattened letter 'v'.
Water start A method of getting underway in which the sailor is pulled out of the water by the rig.
Wetted area The part of the hull in contact with the water.
Wind shift A shift in the direction of the wind.
Windward The direction from which the wind is blowing.
Wings Indentations on the sides of a board used to narrow the tail.
Wiping out Falling (usually dramatically).
Wishbone Another name for the two-sided boom.

INDEX

Numbers in *italics* refer to captions